I Just Got Elected—Now What?
A New Union Officer's Handbook
3rd Edition

DANGER

EDUCATED
UNION MEMBER

By Bill Barry

I Just Got Elected—Now What? A New Union Officer's Handbook 3rd Edition, ©2007, 2014, 2020 Bill Barry. This book was first published by Union Communication Services, Inc., in 2007 and was revised in 2014 and in 2019. Some material in this book previously appeared in *The Steward Update*, a publication of Union Communications Services (UCS).
Published in 2020 by Hard Ball Press
Book formatting for printing by D. Bass
ISBN: 978-1-7344938-1-8
Library of Congress Control Number 2010924576

If you have any comments on the book, please send them along to me at:
4204 Elsrode Ave.
Baltimore, MD 21214
billbarry21214@gmail.com

Other books by the same author

Union Strategies for Hard Times

The 1877 Railroad Strike in Baltimore

From First Contact to First Contract: A Union Organizer's Handbook

Closing Up the Open Shop: A Guide to Internal Organizing (3rd Edition)

Don't Trump on Us: Making Our Unions Great Again

All We Do is Talk Steel: Oral Histories of Sparrows Point (Vol. 1)

PREFACE

There are two vital roles people try to fill without any training: being a parent and being a new union officer. In both cases, they rely on their own experience and hope for the best. Some people realize, however, that the world is changing so quickly that they actually need to study up on how to be better at their roles.

New local union officers enter the world at a very dangerous time and they must deal with situations that are constantly changing, involving both the employers and the unions. Nonetheless, brave workers step forward to take up this challenge of defending themselves, their co-workers and their communities—the toughest job at the toughest time.

We better change the way we do things—or else!

This book has been created to help you out. The lessons here will urge you to change yourselves as well as the union around you, so it won't be easy. Just remember the numbers, however, which demonstrate that your union and unionism in general are in bad shape so there is nowhere to go but up!

This book was originally developed and expanded for those new union officers—and some incumbents—who over many years attended the New Officers Class, part of the Labor Studies Program at The Community College of Baltimore County-Dundalk. Each worker came with hopes of becoming a better union officer. This material, originally on scraps of paper or blackboard diagrams, evolved from their class discussions. These union leaders/students helped to test-drive the material and their participation has been essential. They really wrote this book. I just arranged the material.

Many participants have remained friends and supporters for years, so for the good ones—the ones with heart, spirit and belief in the workers' movement—this book's for you. Thanks for all the great things you do.

Some of my participants turned away, thinking that election to union office was an end in itself and were swallowed up in the old union structure. For those workers who lost their way, this book is a reminder of broken promises.

Thanks to David Prosten, Debbie Wilson, Kathy McCarty, Mike Levene, and to Linda Donahue, Alice Torres and Chris Rolling, who helped produce the several editions, and to Timothy Sheard, who supported this one. A special thanks to Paul Cameron, elected to be Business Manager for IBEW Local 459 in Johnstown, PA, who passed on pages of challenges he encountered as a new officer and to Dharma Noor, who was a new officer at a Newspaper Guild local in Baltimore, who made some very shrewd suggestions. Peter Szilárd Karácsony, an extraordinary union warrior in Budapest, provided many improvements as he developed a new officers program in Hungary. And finally, lotsa love from Dad to Joan, Willie and Alex.

CONTENTS

1 GETTING STARTED

"Be careful what you wish for, you might get it.
Be careful when you run for union office—you might get elected."

—The Great Authority

If there was ever an organization tied to the past, it is the local union. The only organization slower to change is the International Union. If you understand The Servicing Model of Unionism [*Appendix 1*], you will understand that unions—like most organizations today—are leadership-driven: a few people make decisions for the whole group. While this is the accepted structure for a corporation, for a social movement like unionism, the narrowing of power has a destructive effect. As a result, unions generally resist change because the leadership sees change as a threat, and the higher up you go in the union, the more the officers fear change, so even when the numbers show that we are failing, nothing changes—until you got elected to office.

Now you confront a hard decision: were you elected as a union officer to create as few waves as possible, to be timid about starting new programs because you are afraid of making a mistake? If you believe that you should do what has always been done, simply because it has always been done that way, don't waste your time reading this book.

If you ran for office and are looking at making changes to do a better job representing your members, read on.

A word of caution: one new officer pointed out that this book basically covered new officers coming into existing locals, but union organizing programs now mean that new officers are coming into new locals, and basically have to create all of the functions from scratch. As a new officer in one of these locals, you won't have to confront the years of bad union practices but you will need to learn a lot of new things. It is also even more important to emphasize an education program for every worker covered by your contract since unionism is all new to most of them—and to you.

Union locals in the 21st century come in many shapes and sizes. There are the traditional manufacturing industry locals, which often "service" contracts on their own. There are building trades locals that administer a hiring hall and an apprenticeship program and have substantial benefit funds. There are public sector unions whose philosophies, histories, and legal restrictions are very different. There are locals that negotiate their own contracts and settle their own grievances. There are locals that are part of a large

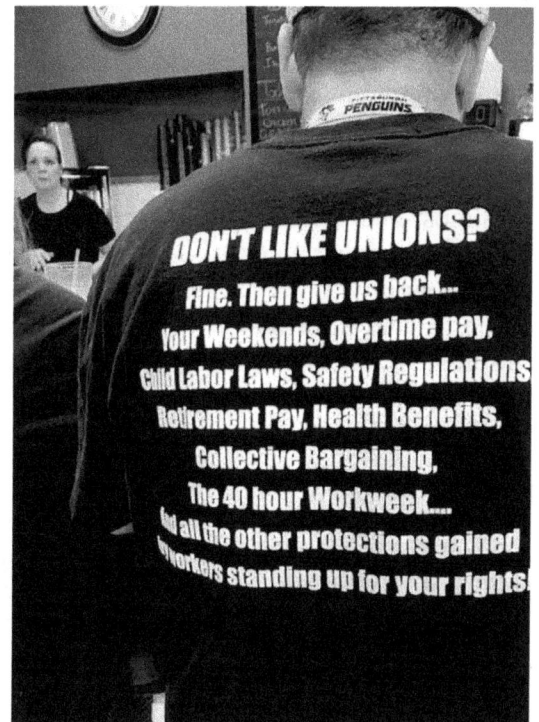

DON'T LIKE UNIONS?
Fine. Then give us back...
Your Weekends, Overtime pay,
Child Labor Laws, Safety Regulations
Retirement Pay, Health Benefits,
Collective Bargaining,
The 40 hour Workweek....
And all the other protections gained
by workers standing up for your rights!

national bargaining structure whose contract and grievances are resolved at the national level far from the local union. There are amalgamated locals, which administer many separate contracts, often in different industries. Importantly, there are new locals, as some unions have successfully expanded organizing campaigns.

The structures of local unions are constantly changing because some international unions, supposedly to put money aside for organizing, have consolidated smaller locals into larger ones, and larger ones into regional structures. Sometimes these changes are initiated by local officers, but often the changes are forced upon a local by higher union officials. In many ways, however, the more things change, the more they stay the same. The local union is still the basic unit of American unionism and the unit closest to the members (and, in open shop states, the non- members). Unions today may often appear different and diverse, but there are common functions and common problems.

One constant of the local union is local elections, which range from bitterly contested to can-we-find-any-one-for-this-office? While no one keeps an accurate count, there seems to be more turnover in union office as longtime veterans of unions' strong days retire, as new locals are organized and as discontented members run for union office, instead of just griping loudly.

There are certain common issues for newly elected officers who try to absorb as much as they can, as quickly as possible, often facing opposition from their own co-workers, from officers who may not have supported their election—and certainly from our employers, who resent stronger unions.

This book was developed for New Officers Training courses to help them—and you. You ran for office because you and many of your co-workers were unhappy with the way the union was functioning, or not functioning. You resented not being informed of decisions. You thought the boss was always getting over on the workers in ways both large—like, bad contracts—and small—like, an endless refusal to settle grievances. You figured that many of the officers simply didn't respond to the concerns of the membership and your members agreed with you.

In almost every case, as a new union officer you first ran against *The Servicing Model of Unionism*, even though you never heard of it or heard it called that. The chart in Appendix 1, contrasts *The Servicing Model of Unionism* with *The Organizing Model*. The Servicing Model, most common in unions today, concentrates authority and information within a small circle of people. In some cases, local union officers even overlap informally with some low level bosses, as if there is a conspiracy. One element of this conspiracy is to keep the same officers in power for as long as possible. That's where you—as a new union officer—have challenged the structure.

The Organizing Model is exactly the opposite and emphasizes Maximum Membership Participation. You may have to almost reinvent unionism in your workplace, bringing changes that could meet with considerable opposition from some of the other officers, your members and, of course, from the boss. In the process, you will have to reinvent yourself, acquiring new knowledge and new skills, making new friends and losing some old ones.

It is also essential to recognize that a local union does not exist in isolation. Union officers and members cannot simply declare a new day for the union and head in the direction they wish. Unions are defined by their relations with employers; after all, the first function of a union is to give workers collective strength and power in dealing with a boss. For this reason, most employers resist unionism and will fight against any improvements you want to make in your local.

Local unions are also defined by their relations with other levels of their own union—the district, the international—and with other unions and with their communities. One challenge for many new officers whose contract is part of a national agreement, is that grievances that start at the local level are resolved by a district or international, usually with no control by the local officers who have to deal with the angry members whose grievances are dropped. In one instance, national union officers forced a revote on a contract that the affected members had decisively turned down. In some building trades unions, international reps may step into local negotiations, claiming "national patterns" to force locals to accept regressive contract language. In one instance in Baltimore, a local union was successfully sued by employers for almost $4 million for conducting a strike over local issues after the national contract was settled.

All of these changes have to take place at a tough time in history: the global economy is creating havoc in workplaces all across the United States, and anti-unionism is rampant and brazen. There is an enormous separation in wealth between the ruling class and the workers, supported by a culture that glorifies the robber barons of the new millennium. There is no question that the "game" has really changed for union officers over the past 30 years—longstanding companies have been taken over by venture capitalists, with only short-term profits as a goal. Negotiations are all about takeaways and concessions, not about improvements. Politicians who used to ask for labor support now run campaigns to attack and vilify public sector unions. A real crisis is that, over and over, longtime union officers have been left behind, unable to deal with these changes. They approach negotiations, for example, as if it were the sunny 1970's, unprepared for attacks by management representatives who attend special workshops on how to shred unions.

As classes for New Local Union Officers were offered, it became clear that the officers who *really* needed some guidance and skill often refused to attend. The attitude of ignorance, of an officer who turns away from education and improvement, is one of the gravest problems in the culture of modern unionism. Many union officers at all levels resist any training, especially if they have to go on their own time or pay for the education out of their own pockets. They simply follow the path that has been laid out for them, even if the numbers show that the path is leading their union into oblivion.

And so here you are! A brave new officer, thinking that you may have signed on as an officer on the Titanic for its first voyage. There is no doubt that you have accepted a challenge at a time of crisis for the workers' movement in the United States.

One reflection of the disconnect that is fundamental to the Servicing Model is the constant happy talk from high union officers about the resurgence of unions, contrasted to the abysmally low membership. At the Maryland-DC AFL-CIO convention in November, 2019, AFL-CIO Secretary-Treasurer Liz Shuler proclaimed that a Gallup poll found that 64% of Americans "favor unions," but, according to figures from the Department of Labor [*Appendix 3*], union membership in the private sector in 2018 was 6.4%, the lowest percentage since 1900, and overall membership, at 10.5%, is comparable to that of 1910.So, unionism has been pushed back more than 100 years, an absolute catastrophe.

John Sweeney, former president of the AFL-CIO, astutely warned in a speech to the AFL-CIO Executive Board in February, 2001, that unions may not exist as "a viable institution" if the membership decline is not reversed. These words are even more true today. Numbers do count, and the abrupt decline in union membership, in union density (as a percentage of the workforce, or "market share"), and in union political influence since Sweeney's ominous prediction is written large on the wall for everyone to see.

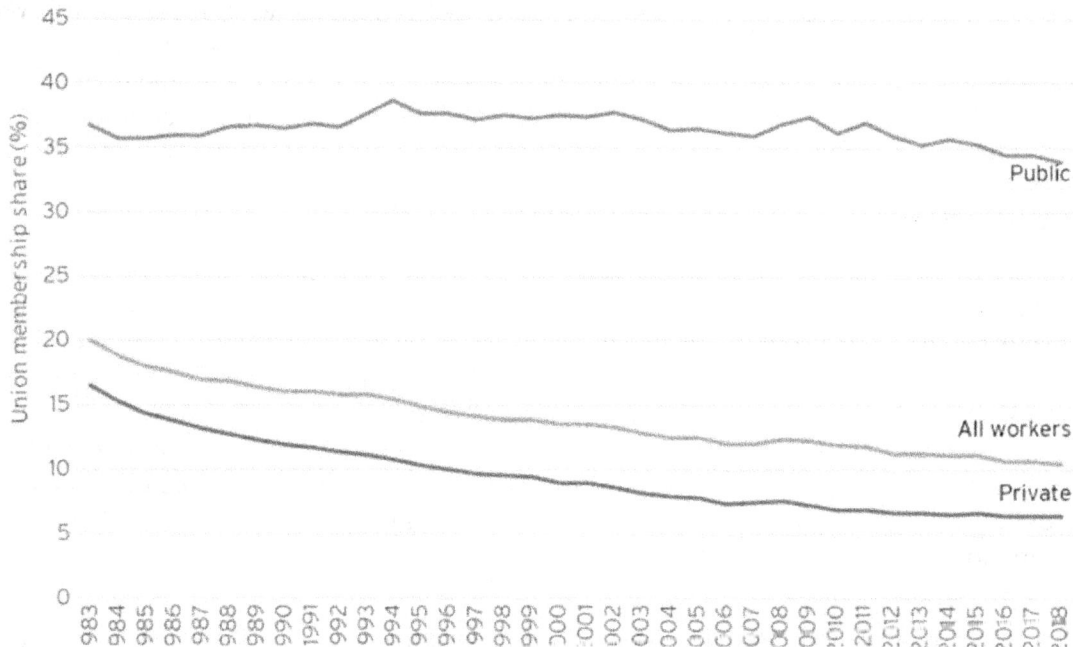

Companies are investing billions of dollars to train us for our workplace jobs, recognizing that new technology and processes make the workplace an ever-changing and ever-expanding universe. Business schools stress that companies which refuse to change are commercial dinosaurs. The structure of unionism—broken up into competing craft union jurisdictions or burdened with national and nonfunctional units—has been an attempt to adapt 19th-century organizations to 21st-century economic realities. It doesn't work and the annual membership figures show that unionism, for various reasons, is in drastic decline in this country.

If unionism in the U.S. is going to grow, the challenges for existing unions, and for the non-union workers who want representation, are enormous. Needed changes are both external—organizing millions of new members—and internal—changes in how existing unions operate at every level. While Sweeney tried almost 20 years ago to bully the various unions into starting new organizing programs, there was general resistance to this change. Organizing is enormously expensive; it requires a whole new group of skilled staff people and it meets enormous social and legal challenges.

Let's look inward, however, at a problem which affects you as a new local union officer—internal organization. The level of participation in the union "movement" is pathetically low. Although no one has actually tried to measure the rate of membership involvement, experience shows that only about 3% to 5% of union members regularly participate in union activities. Oh sure, if there is a contract ratification everyone shows up but often the hall is empty for years at a time and you have a difficult time getting a quorum to pass any motions.

More importantly, workers who don't want to participate in the union are able to simply drop out and become free riders—taking all of the benefits, of course, but not paying dues. The revival of the open shop movement over the past five years has increased the number of open shop (mislabeled "right-to-work") states to 27 (plus Guam), and the Supreme Court decision, *Janus v. AFSCME,* cut into public sector unions' ability to collect "fair share" fees from non-members.

Needless to say, some union officers seldom express much concern about the low level of union membership participation because more union participation inevitably leads to challenges in union elections—and we can't have that, can we?

One issue related to The Servicing Model of Unionism is what we will call the "Old Joe" theory. "Old Joe" is the longtime local president who developed his own way of doing things over the years, often without much planning or thought—things just kind of happened. If you were a member of the local, you figured that's the way things have always been done, and maybe we should keep on. When confronted with a challenge, often members will complain: "But we've never done it that way." This became the "Old Joe" theory, which new local officers have to confront before making improvements in their locals. Officers simply passed experience down from one generation to the next, without much effort to learn new and different ways, as if we only learned to cook by watching our parents and never checked into a cookbook.

CHANGE. This word is essential and yet it is the word no one wants to whisper at a union meeting. Our bosses have been told by *their* bosses: if you do not change, you will die. They repeat this mantra in negotiations as a rationale for reducing job classifications, or for subcontracting, or for demanding concessions. Flexibility. Unfettered flexibility. The bosses claim that they are accountable to the stockholders, to higher corporate management, to the marketplace, to the taxpayers. In each case, they insist that there are standards that they must meet or else the enterprise will disappear. Indeed, this threat of extinction drives most corporate decisions whose impact, of course, falls most heavily on local union members.

Once upon a time, some large corporations accepted unionism as a fact of life and even used the union as a method for controlling the workforce. Favorable contract clauses, such as union security, dues check-off, lost time and special status, were granted to "responsible" unions and their officers—those that would maintain discipline on the floor as strictly as any supervisor.

In general, however, bosses today want to move fast and furious and consider the union an obstacle. After all, why be bogged down in negotiations over plant closings or privatization or new work assignments with that stupid ol' union? Without a union, the boss can simply make his moves and get on with it. Workers without unions have been brainwashed into a sense of powerlessness. This sense of futility is often reinforced by former union members with their sad tales of plant closings and concessions—a ragged landscape in which "the union didn't do anything."

In the public sector, the same approach has brought on significant challenges to unions. Demands to privatize, to cut benefits such as pensions or sick leave, and to prolong negotiations have become common. Change is everywhere—anti-union forces out-organized us and the very existence of unions is now an issue in many states, which had once accepted unionism in the public sector.

The need to change is equally true for unionism so that we can respond to these attacks. Only the membership can begin to make these changes, which involve a lot more than simply replacing officers in a structure that doesn't work. Many union officers don't really understand change and, if they do, they fear it. They cling to the status quo because the status quo means their continued position in union office.

In an ideal world there would be rational standards and objectives for every organization—corporations, political structures and unions—to drive these organizations to improvement. Alas, capitalism is far from a perfect world, so we must fall back upon the realities of local union structures and politics and hope for—and expect—the best.

This is the best argument for *change* in unions, and it is also one of the first lessons for a new local union officer: if something isn't working, why keep doing it over and over? You got elected because the membership was unhappy with the status quo, so don't simply sit.

Fortunately, not all of these changes are negative—there has been an enormous increase in union militancy. At the end of 2019, it is clear that members are demanding something better—49,000 UAW members were on strike at GM, 25,000 teachers and support staff struck in Chicago, 3,600 UAW members struck Mack Trucks and in 2018, nearly 500,000 workers struck, the highest number in 15 years. More importantly, our non-members have been caught up in this new surge. In the open shop state of Arizona, for example, there are 90,000 certified teachers but only about 20,000 (22%) were members of the Arizona Education Association. When it came time to vote in April, 2018, on a strike for both increased salaries and more spending on public schools, 57,000 (63%) filled out a ballot, and a poll showed that 78% of the teachers supported the strike.

The chapters of this book deal with different areas of concern for the new union officer and include a set of tasks at the end of each chapter—practical things that you need to do, possibly with your co-workers or other officers, to get your local union straightened out. It will help if you write out both the questions and the possible answers as a way of improving your self-discipline.

Now Go Do It!

TASKS:

)What were the issues in your local that helped you get elected?

2)What kind of campaign organization did you put together?

3)What experience do you already have in your union?

4)How involved are your members in their union?

5)What are the most important changes your union needs to make?

6)Who can you count on to help you make these changes?

7)What obstacles to change do you think you will encounter?

2 UNDERSTANDING THE ORGANIZING MODEL OF UNIONISM

"Too long have the workers of the world waited for some Moses to lead them out of bondage. I would not lead you out if I could; for if you could be led out, you could be led back again. I would have you make up your minds there is nothing that you cannot do for yourselves." Eugene Debs (1905)

Let's look again at two models for union operation—The Servicing Model and The Organizing Model—in *Appendix 1*—that illustrate two very different ways of operating a union. Go through each line of each model and see which items apply to your local union. In 1995, when John Sweeney ran for president of the AFL-CIO—as, you got it, an insurgent candidate—he made popular the expression "organizing model of unionism." Diagrams began to appear as if by magic, and some excellent theories of revitalizing unions became real. Union members at all levels, leadership and rank-and-file alike, began to look at how things got done and how we got where we are. Even though Sweeney has been gone from office, the term is still kicked around, even if most union officers won't practice what they preach.

The Organizing Model represents, in a way, a process called "Back to the Future," in which unionism of the 21st century resembles unionism of the 19th century, when it was totally driven by the membership, and had to fight for every gain against enormous opposition from both the bosses and the government.

In the days when unions were active and growing, the full membership's participation was needed to build power to take on some of the most vicious anti-union SOB's in history. Union members lacked the conveniences that are common today: dues check-off, full-time union staff and officers, union halls, money in the bank. Everything that the union did, the members and their supporters had to do for themselves. They had to talk about the union with each other at work and in their communities.

Because unions were struggling, members realized the importance of involving their families and their neighbors in their battles. As they looked around for help, they found it outside their own membership: in their communities, with organizations like churches, ethnic social groups and neighborhood associations. Union members understood the importance of growth through organizing, and who better to describe the advantages of being in a union than a worker who had recently organized?

In his wonderful memoir about growing up in a union family, Jack Metzgar wrote in *Striking Steel: Solidarity Remembered* about his father's organizing efforts in the steel industry. The improvements were so dramatic that his father's life was divided in two distinct periods: before the union and after the union.

All of this history may seem ancient, but a new union officer can look at these activities and get some excellent guidance on how to increase membership involvement today. The old-timers, as we often call them, knew something. After all, they helped build the labor movement. In fact, one great resource for you are your union retirees—get them to tell you how they built the union from the beginning and you can see what worked. You could even post interviews with some of the retirees on your local union web page (and your local union WILL get a web page) so younger members can get a sense of important union history—how they got the benefits they have today.

Speaking of old-timers, one new officer urged his local to support a New Unionists committee to encourage the next generation of officers to get involved now. There has been a sporadic national effort through the AFL-CIO to encourage participation by these younger members with groups like the Young Trade Unionists, attached to central labor councils. These groups were often dependent upon the energies of an individual, or small group and are regularly challenged by inertia, reduced hiring and, honestly, opposition from entrenched union officers who fear the involvement of new blood.

Over time and for a variety of reasons that are beyond the scope of this book, The Servicing Model of Unionism developed and has continued virtually unchanged and unchallenged since the mid-1940s—beyond the lifetimes of most union members today. In the Servicing Model, a few people make all of the decisions while the majority of members wait passively for good result.

As a new officer, you will quickly see that management has a very definite interest in controlling the election of local officers. Management wants someone they "can work with"—that is, who is willing to allow management to "be competitive," to "run the business (or public agency) without interference" and who will merge the interests of the union with those of the business. Moreover, management by its very nature controls, by my estimate, about one-third of your members in any local election and is not afraid to use its muscle to sway the votes. You may be shocked to find that some of the officers regularly hang out in the personnel office or accept gifts from management.

Isn't that why you ran for office?

As we discussed in Chapter 1, union membership—defined as dues-payers—is pitifully low, and the even more chilling figure is the low level of involvement of members in their unions. In the states where it is legal to negotiate a union security clause, workers belong to the union because it is required under the terms of their union contract, as a condition of employment. Does this make you a union "member" in the true sense? Not really. These members think, with their dues, they are simply buying a service, like cable TV. When the service goes out—a lousy contract, grievances not settled—it is common for a member to sit back and complain—loudly!!—that all The Union does is collect dues. The sense of the members that "The Union" is separate from them is the most fundamental element of The Servicing Model of Unionism.

These "members" regard The Union as a third party, somewhere between themselves and the boss—a helpful insurance plan, but not an organization worth supporting. The list of complaints is long and, in many cases, justified. As a result, only about 3-5% of union members are "active"—that is, they are officers, or stewards or participate on union committees.

In a perverse way, a union in an open shop state can give a more accurate description because workers not only stop participating in the union but actually can drop out. In the year since the *Janus* decision, the numbers of non-members have become clear—and it's scary. In Maryland, for example, there are 74,000 teachers across the state, with 3,000 agency fee payers before the *Janus* decision. With about 18,000 non-members state-wide, about 28% of teachers covered by an MTA contract are free riders.

So why change? Because we are in big trouble, that's why! Current figures present disastrous conditions for unions and an even more frightening future. The numbers show unionism in the new century faces a many-sided crisis, so that just staying the course is no longer an option. So, the member comes to a fork in the road. One path leads to greater indifference or anti-unionism—to never participating, to constant complaining and maybe to dropping out of the union. The other path, which you obviously took, is to shoulder the weight of leadership and get ready for changes. As Henry Ford famously said: "Don't find fault—find a remedy. Anybody can complain."

You also have to understand what I call "The Savior Mentality"—people believe that, in politics or in the union, there is a magical and easy solution to all of our problems. As we saw in the elections of Donald Trump in 2016, with support from 47% of union voters, and the victory of Boris Johnson and the Conservatives in England in 2019, workers want some charismatic figure who can wave a magic wand and make everything right—poof!—as if one person can turn the world around.

This attitude, based upon the unwillingness of people to put time and effort into social change, is a flop, so don't duplicate it in your union planning. This is especially true for you as a new officer because it is unreasonable for your supporters to expect immediate miracles. You cannot turn around a situation overnight that took years to build up—while the members simply sit back and cheer—or boo, depending on the moment.

It's the attitude you have to challenge.

This chapter concerns the fundamental way the local union should operate. If you got elected as an insurgent candidate—that is, without the support of the good-old-boy network (which often includes women)—then you already know the importance of membership involvement. You have also figured out how to rouse the membership, the sleeping giant, at least to the extent of getting them out to vote for you. It is so important to use the excitement and momentum of your election campaign "by coming up with member social activities and getting really busy getting our feet under us," as one new officer described it, emphasizing that you also have to switch from "campaign mode to being responsible for the members and their families."

Now you have to accept *maximum membership involvement* in the future as a positive thing for your union. If you don't, your election will not improve the union at all. You may get re-elected if that is your desire, but you will not become an outstanding union leader. You will be merely another tired copy of the officer you replaced, and unionism, as a whole, will continue to circle the drain in the United States, illustrating the famous quotation from management guru W. Edwards Deming: "The only reason an organization has dead wood is that management either hired dead wood or it hired live wood and killed it."

A publicly held company that experiences huge losses in sales and revenue, and a horrendous drain on its resources and assets, would be exposed to public scrutiny. Stockholders and investors, at least, would be screaming for change. In a union, the stockholders are the members, but they have separated themselves from any knowledge of the union as a whole, concentrating on such essential personal issues as: do I have a job, will I be getting overtime this week, can I make all of my bills this month?

Very few union members raised the alarm, certainly not the officers of the various unions that make up the AFL-CIO. Most of them were experiencing dramatic declines in membership, loss of bargaining power and erosion of conditions, but admitting that the emperor has no clothes would expose every one of them to the threat of overthrow. The negative dynamic of union leadership is to resist and to resent change, which threatens the incumbent officers, despite some of the rhetoric.

A deeper question is whether building the union or expanding its membership is worth doing. Many union officers don't seem to think so. I have seen many officers who sit around and dream about increased membership or at least more dues income, but never worry about how to make it happen. After all, in today's anti-union atmosphere in the United States, a boss is unlikely to show up at the door of the union hall and beg to sign a contract. As we will see in Chapter 4, most unions are not devoting the resources needed for an extensive new organizing program to rebuild both sheer numbers plus bargaining power in core industries.

If you accept membership involvement as a positive thing for the union, now you have to make it happen. Knowing your starting point is a good idea, so you can judge whether you are making any progress. In some ways, the measurement is easy because it is driven by sheer numbers: the more members who turn out for a particular activity, the better. There are several ways to run each function of your union, so making maximum membership participation an important element is really a dramatic change. Every activity will be run differently as a result.

To get yourself started in transforming your union, the first thing to do is to make a list of all of the activities of the union (and you may need to refer to Chapter 4 to get a list of the union's functions) and rate each one (1 for "high" to 5 for "low") according to its membership involvement. Do not give any particular activity a value judgment at this point. For example, do not ignore the large numbers of members who may participate in union social or athletic activities, contrasted to the meager numbers who show up to leaflet for a political candidate or who volunteer to run for union office. Every union activity is both important and instructional because it shows you how members can be attracted to union activities.

In most organizations, like unions, Little League or church or social groups, only about 3% of the membership takes an active role in maintaining the organization. If you have ever coached your children's team, you know what I am talking about. Remember the parents who barely slow down enough to drop their kids out of their cars and never spend a moment helping with the team? Too busy! Gotta be someplace! Somehow the program continues, thanks to the dedication of a small group of parents but you, as an active participant, seethe with anger and resentment over their lack of participation.

As a new officer, you should look around in your own life at how these other organizations—churches, fraternal organizations, the PTA, Little League teams—try to increase membership and raise money. Look at the ones that are successful and see what worked. Look at the ones that are slipping into oblivion and avoid their mistakes.

You must understand that you will meet some opposition from the members themselves. The Organizing Model of Unionism requires not only that the union officers change the way they do things, but it also forces the members to change dramatically. Union membership will no longer be a spectator sport. Members will have to learn the contract, will have to attend meetings, will have to make decisions, may even have to take some risks. Each of these involves a lot of time, a lot of work and sometimes becomes a royal pain. Most workers think they can be successful by being obedient: follow orders, don't rock the boat. As a result, they often find it difficult to make the complicated decisions that face today's unions.

A while back there was an interesting exchange via the internet among some UAW members who were unhappy with the direction of both their local unions and the International Union. When one member lamented the difficulties of getting the members together for a strike or some sort of large-scale action, another member replied that the members were unhappy and could be expected to vote accordingly in the next local election.

This is not good enough today. Don't let your members think that it's enough to show up every three or four years to vote for some candidate—even you!—who is supposedly going to change the union. There is a parallel movement in politics: if all citizens do is participate every couple of years by voting, is it any surprise that major issues—the decline of our living standards, the issue of economic inequality or the repeated attacks on unionism for example—are rarely debated? Once upon a time, the unions were a movement—every day of the year. The Organizing Model of Unionism requires that we put the movement back into unionism. You have to challenge each of your members to truly be a member, not just a dues-payer.

Remember one important point: we have no choice. Look at the numbers, which show that we are approaching extinction, especially in the private sector. A whole generation has come into our workplaces as children of

Reaganomics, trained in schools and in society to oppose collective action. If we don't organize young work-

Now Go Do It!

TASKS:

1) Evaluate your local in terms of the chart on The Servicing Model of Unionism. Carefully go over each item and discuss it in your union. How do your officers and your members fit into the scheme?

2) Has your local union gained or lost members in the past five years? How about your international union? The district or region?

3) Evaluate all of the functions of your local in terms of membership involvement.

4) Do you think that grievances are being properly handled in your workplace?

5) How successful were your last contract negotiations?

ers of every generation, the unions may die.

3 INDIVIDUAL CHANGES
"Be the change you want to see."
Mahatma Gandhi

Change is like charity—it begins at home. As you begin to plan the reorganization of the union, let's not forget where new organization really begins: with you, the new officer. In some ways, this chapter should be the first one in this book because if you do not change and grow, then all of your efforts to change others will flop. As you struggle and scheme to create new membership activities, you will have to dramatically change your attitude and activities to make the campaign successful.

New union officers who were students in my classes made it clear to me that this chapter was more important than I first expected. After all, eager members who ran for office would certainly bring change once they got into office—wouldn't they? A disappointing aftermath of a local union election is the candidate who had shown an enormous burst of energy and organization, and then, after being elected, acts as if getting to the top of the mountain was enough and sits down to rest for a year or so.In some cases, a new officer elected alone simply didn't have the True Grit to constantly challenge hostile officers. In some other cases, regrettably, the new officer figured out that getting time off the floor for union business was a lovely luxury and if some compromises had to be made to protect this new position of privilege, so be it.

Many readers of this book remarked that the changes they had to make in their lives were as important, and as difficult, as the changes in dealing with their bosses. Some even created self-assessment tests for all of the union officers, helping them to focus on areas where they felt they needed improvement and then reached out to get them the necessary training. This training can be complex—like how to present an arbitration—or mundane—like learning how to type! One Teamster officer remarked that "The Organizing Model is nice, but we have elected business agents who did not have basic typing skills. The Organizing Model does not get an information request written."

Look at the chart on union leadership [*Appendix 4*] for a checklist in this area.. As an officer, you must show the same energy and focus on organization, and the same proactive attitude, after the election that you demonstrated during your campaign. The most important change is constant learning, a new process for many officers who have "learned" how to handle grievances, for example, by watching older, more experienced

union officers, like Old Joe. Our world is dramatically changing and there is a relentless, and well-funded, surge of anti-unionism. Private sector companies are being bought, sold and flipped, bringing new management and disrupting long-term relations. The public sector has been drastically privatized, bringing the same vicious anti-unionism into federal and state labor relations.

We call it Best Union Practices. All across the country—and around the world—workers and new union officers are figuring out how to deal with these changes. You need to know what they are doing—where they have been successful and where they have failed, so that you can benefit from their wins and learn from their losses. It is particularly disappointing to see officers who claim they can't find the time to read or hear from other officers who make the same mistakes, or fall into the same traps, as the officers they defeated. Unionism is in a crisis and we have to have a sense of urgency to meet the challenges. So we, as individuals, have to reinvent ourselves.

It also can be a great collective effort, especially if you came into office as part of a slate. Divide up the "new learning" assignments so that everyone has a piece that can be shared at meetings or posted on a website. Has a law changed? You need to know about it. Has a union won, or lost, key contract language? You need to be aware of the changes. Has a union on the other side of the country figured out a slick scheme to build leverage? Has a steward in Ireland, or India, or Mexico, who works for your same company figured a way to confront anti-unionism? You need to figure if it could work for your local as well. Create a site for Best Union Practices and keep adding to it.

What changes do you have to make?

•*Positive focus is essential.* In many ways, when you ran for office you ran a negative campaign—the incumbents you challenged were doing things wrong, so you criticized them. OK, your campaign worked, so now you are the incumbent. You have to change your thinking so that you can develop a program for moving your local in a positive direction. You may find this a very difficult adjustment because being negative, or running a negative campaign, is the easiest thing in the world. Anyone can sit at the back of the union meeting and throw tomatoes at the officers.

You could play to all of the fears and prejudices of your members and used the cynicism and distrust that many members have for "The Union"—as if it were separate from them—to get elected. Now you have to dramatically turn things around. You must fight to get these same distrusting members to put their time and their energies and their trust into rebuilding their union. Creating an Action Plan for your local, as described in Chapter 4, is a basic part of this change.

As you begin to change, and your local begins to change and you are buffeted by cruel economic and political

winds from outside, it may seem like it is impossible to ever get control of any situation but stick with it and you will do well.

• **Be well organized yourself.** You can't organize others if you are not organized yourself. Here are some tools to make it happen:

1) Get yourself a couple of legal pads that will be used only for union activities, keep them with you at all times and mark them To-Do. One pad should be marked "Reactive" and will include everything you do in response to management, or to requests from your members. The other pad will be marked "Proactive," and will list the projects you want to start. Both of these pads will remind you of all of the things that need to get done (members you need to contact, information you need to get, meetings you need to schedule or to attend—the list will be a very long one).

1) If you are fortunate enough to have a union office, or even a union desk, make sure to keep it well organized. Figure out a filing system—either paper or electronic/computer—and work to make sure that you do not have piles of material all over the place. One new union officer said that she put sticky notes around her desk of things she needed to do.Not good organizing. Not only will you lose stuff, or waste a lot of time looking for it, you will *look* disorganized to your members, hardly a quality to build their confidence. Remember what you tell your kids: a place for everything and everything in its place. It works for new union officers as well.

2) Write everything down. You can't keep everything in your head so don't even try. Careful lists and outlines will help keep you on track, so your members will respect you as focused and not forgetful. If you had decent steward's training, you would have learned about The Steward's Tool Box, the folder that every steward should have containing all union materials (contracts, bylaws, grievance forms, fact sheets, organizing leads, political action notes, etc.).

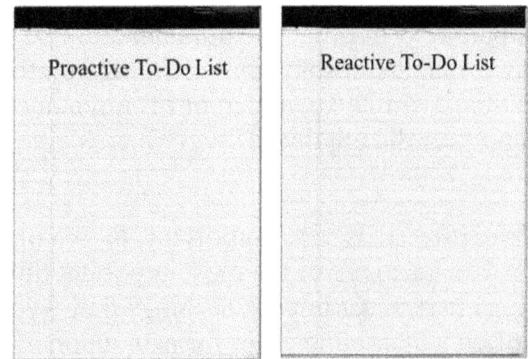

•**Proactive attitude.** Do you feel that, as a new union officer, you are walking on an endless sidewalk covered with ice? You can never get your footing and you keep slipping and falling backwards. A reactive attitude leaves you in this position, constantly pushed by outside forces who make you deal with their issues rather than the ones you choose to build the union.

Obviously, this whole process of change involves an attitude adjustment. If you are constantly reacting to events, or letting your boss decide what issues the union will have to deal with, then you are never going to turn your union around. 'Nuff said.

When you are proactive, you expect to make things happen. You pick the issues and define the debates that will build the union and actively involve your members (and help you sign up the non-members). A reactive effort is one forced upon you and your union and is often a defensive battle, one that may divide your members from each other and from the community of workers around you.

As part of your proactive attitude, don't be so afraid of making a wrong decision that you become paralyzed, so worried about someone ridiculing you for a mistake that you become overly cautious and eventually indecisive. As Ed Duke, a mentor of mine, once said: "The only person who never made a mistake was the one who never did anything."

•*Prioritize*. It is also important, as we mentioned in the chapter on Strategic Planning, to set priorities so that you take care of the most important things first. Let the little stuff wait until you have enough time. First things first, most important things first—you know all of the clichés. Like most clichés, this one is true and is often a stumbling point for new union officers. All issues are *not* of equal importance; the skill is in evaluating a situation to decide its importance. If you treat all situations as equally important, you will be running around in circles. One method for establishing priorities is to look at a problem in terms of membership involvement: how many members are affected and therefore could be involved. If the numbers are large, go for it.

• *Delegate responsibility*. As you begin to consider activities for the local union, always base your planning on increasing the involvement of your membership. This simple principle will turn your union around. It is easier to talk about than to accomplish, and it will require that you continue to develop your organizing skills. Many projects that you consider will require

! DELEGATE !

all of the strategic decisions covered in Chapter 4. Often it is faster, more efficient and easier for you to make the decisions and to carry them out yourself—a project gets done right, and on time.

But. . . how many members have been involved in carrying the project out? None, or at least no new ones. So when you start a project, you should always reach out to your members and get them involved. Asking them to "get involved" won't work because this plea is too vague and open-ended. Give a member some specific tasks to follow through, share your sense of strategic planning, and soon you will have members who can, and hopefully will, step up to work on their own. They will develop skills and confidence and—whoops—they just might decide to run for office! Get ready for it and get used to it. After all, that's where you came from.

Make this membership involvement one of your main goals. Here's a trick: in your notebook or in your computer, keep track of which members you have involved in a union project, and how they performed. The longer your list, the better you are doing as a new officer.

Keep in touch with each of them as a part of your To Do list and you will soon see a change in the union. By the way, the people you reach are also people you can come back to for help in another election campaign, so all this activity is not just charity.

Steps to effective time management

1. Long term vision.
2. Prioritization.
3. Scheduling.
4. Delegation.
5. Improve concentration.
6. Being well organized.
7. Avoid Procrastination
8. Reduce Interruptions.
9. Efficient Meetings.
10. Effective communication.
11. Avoid perfectionism
12. Be assertive.

Remember—leadership is not what you do, it's what you get others to do.

•*Manage Your Time*. As part of being well organized, your time management skills will be put to the test. There will be many new demands on the hours in your days—local meetings, grievance meetings, political action meetings, central labor council meetings, and caucus meetings. You name it—you are expected to be there. Not only can you feel overwhelmed in your union work, these new demands on your time can create tensions at work and at home. You have to sit down and figure out exactly what the best use of your time is. In some cases, the decisions are easy: skip your regular TV time and start studying up on the union or consolidate some of your shopping. At a more complicated level, get together with the members of your household and see how they will respond to your attending extra night meetings, for example. Like a war, it is essential that the people on the home front support you in your efforts to improve your union. At the same time, as part of the Action Plan, see who else can participate in some of the activities—you get some free time and, more importantly, you get others to be active in their union.

• *Don't Waste Your Time*. Many union activities are gatherings without a point. Beware the schedule of continuous meetings or functions. You will pretty quickly figure out which ones are wastes of time and which ones will help your union grow.

You will also quickly learn how to run an effective meeting by respecting the time demands of your members. If you have a meeting, make sure there is a point to it and a strict time frame, so that important issues can be covered and time is not wasted on petty bickering or on individual grievances. Your membership participation will fall in direct proportion to the length of your meetings. Many times, a member will finally attend a meeting and will be so put off by the activities that he/she will not come back.

•*Hold on to Outside Activities*. Do not forget the importance of *doing something else*. Anything else that will relieve the tension and concentration of your union work is a valuable part of your tight schedule. Family or social activities are still very important.

• *Learn New Things*. As you can see in *Appendix 6,* you have to undergo a change in your personal skills now that you are an officer. You have to become familiar with all of the jobs covered by your contract, with all of the personalities and possible grievances. If you were a department steward, you knew the work in your area because you did it. You knew the personalities and grievances because you lived with them every day. As an officer, you have to develop the same familiarity and one good way is a "listening tour." Go around to every area of your workplace to see what workers do and then ask the stewards and members what problems they confront. You may even want to have private meetings to get more detailed information. You may have to learn another language or deal with a more diverse workforce and membership than you had, for example, as a department steward.

As an officer, you may even be responsible for managing other workers—union staff, for example—and whole new area of skill. This is often the biggest leap, in my experience, and the one with the greatest failure rate. We don't know how to manage ourselves and suddenly we have to manage others as well.

•*Evaluate yourself honestly*. If excuses were money, many union officers would be very wealthy. Once again, you ran a campaign based on promises that officers made and didn't keep, so do not fall into the same trap. Look at Chapter 4, which covers Strategic Planning: one of the most important moves is to set goals and then to realistically check whether you are moving along toward them. You should follow the same process in evaluating your personal progress and be as tough on yourself as you were in your campaign on the incumbent officers. Your members did not elect you so they could listen to a lot of apologies and excuses for things that are not getting done. *In full and on time* should be your motto! A great way to evaluate yourself is to ask: what can we claim as accomplishments over the past month? Two months? Six months? If you can't list some proactive activities, then you need to re-evaluate yourself.

•*Learn to listen*. So many new officers take their positions with an enormously inflated sense of their own skills and importance. As a result, they don't understand how complicated it really is to become a good officer. After all, our bosses train us repeatedly for even the most basic procedures, but new officers often believe that they can function effectively without any kind of apprenticeship. Big mistake. A good quality, which is part of the honest self-evaluation mentioned in the previous paragraph, is to understand what you don't know and that you need to listen carefully to everyone around you. You don't have to believe everything you hear but listen carefully anyway. Make

I Just Got Elected—Now What?

sure your members *know* you are listening carefully—listening to someone else is a sign of respect. And remember this one important point: when you're talking, you're not listening.

•*Learn to speak*. At the same time, you will now be speaking a lot, in many different circumstances. Would you rather have a root canal? Join the crowd. Most of us have dreaded getting up in front of a room full of people, even friendly and familiar ones, but a union officer must be able to "make the pitch," as the expression goes. Once again, you cannot simply make excuses for not being able, or willing, to speak. You just have to learn to do it.

Speakers generally find themselves in front of three kinds of audiences: a large group, a small group, or a one-on-one. If you have run successfully for union office, you have obviously done something right in the speaking department. You could take a short course in public speaking or you can simply try to believe that by being well-prepared you can make a decent presentation on your own. No matter how you do it, do it.

You can use this skill when dealing with the media. Too often, newspaper articles or TV coverage report that "an officer of the union was not available for comment," while giving a full presentation of management's position. Unions live in a world of public opinion so you need to be able—and willing—to make your case.

•*Get as much new information as possible*. As a new local union officer, you may feel like the television character who wails: "It's too much information!" There is no such thing as too much information in the union. You have to set aside time to learn and to study, either on your own or in some Labor Studies class, if one is available in your area.

Make it a priority to get out and talk with officers of other locals from your union (at District or Regional meetings, for example) or with officers of other unions in specific terms about how they handle union challenges. At first you may be disappointed by how *little* many officers think about what they do. They are simply trapped in the Old Joe method of servicing unionism. You ask them a question and they look at you like you're a little loony. Don't be surprised and don't give up. Keep asking and you will eventually find other officers who have figured out ways to build up their unions and who will be willing to share their secrets to success with you.

You will often come into contact with officers from different unions, in different industries or from different geographical areas. Most commonly, you meet up at central labor council functions or political activities. In most cases, officers just show up to respond to the decisions made by some higher officer or to enjoy a social function, but you are on a mission to build your union. Take advantage of these gatherings to find out what other unions are doing. Remember, as a new officer your basic goal is to learn as much as possible about unionism and solidarity. You could also suggest that a district meeting cancel the open bar and reception, substituting a workshop or panel on better grievance handling so everyone can hear how some officers are moving ahead.

You should also look at leadership practices that management follows. In the *New York Times,* for example, there is a weekly column in the Business section in which executives are interviewed about their problems and best practices. Many of their insights—even though some seem crazy—might also apply to your union; they are all devoted to the topic of leadership—just as this book is. Follow these discussions and see if you can pick up any tips.

改
善

KAIZEN

Kai—Change   Zen—Good

"Taking something apart and putting it back together better

It is also important, as we discussed in the first chapter, to keep a written record of anything new that you are learning.

•*Kaizen.* If you never heard this term, your boss missed some of the latest worker control theories. It is a Japanese term meaning "change for the better" or "continuous improvement"—more popularly "take it apart and put it back together better." Bosses are pulled into the idea by the competition in the global marketplace, and even public employers are using it as a way to reduce employment or to improve old practices.

For the workers, *kaizen* always causes trouble because it means your boss is messing with the union contract, cutting away at past practices or increasing the pressure for productivity. *Kaizen* reflects a proactive attitude, an aggressive approach and a sense of constant change that puts your union constantly on the defensive. It is a common feature for executives in fast-moving industries to assert that they never are satisfied with what they know because there is always someone else who knows more. This aggressive attitude toward learning, toward *kaizen*, is probably the single most important individual change you can make in order to become a successful union officer.

Even though the boss may have figured out *kaizen* first, it is still a great principle. You should energetically apply it to your union activities. Look at constantly improving yourself, bringing in new activities, new information and new members.

•***Dealing with Conflict***. Do you hate to fight with people? Most of us do. In fact, many of us have been trained in service industries to act as if someone else—like a customer—is always right. The new activity in your union will inevitably create frictions, and you better get ready for them. In some cases, the frictions are simply passionate disagreements over how to improve the union. In other cases, incumbent officers fear the increase in membership involvement will cut off some of the perks that they have enjoyed and they will fight, like any king or queen, to maintain their position of privilege.

One reader remarked that the most serious internal disputes were started by disgruntled candidates who lost. For them, the campaign was not over and the success of the local was not a consideration, so don't get caught up in their bad situations. As Frederick Douglass so eloquently explained, "If there is no struggle, there is no progress. Those who profess to favor freedom and yet deprecate agitation are men who want crops without plowing up the ground, they want rain without thunder and lightning. They want the ocean without the awful roar of its waves . . ."

So, don't get caught by guilt feelings when someone calls you "a troublemaker" or "an agitator." Accept these labels with pride, if you haven't done so already. Change always brings conflict but try to learn to disagree without being disagreeable. As Herbert Bayard Swope once said, "I cannot give you the formula for success, but I can give you the formula for failure, which is: Try to please everybody."

•***Don't take everything personally.*** If you are going to survive as a new local officer, you will find plenty of problems. Don't react as if everything is directed at you as an individual. You represent change, a new way of running the union, The Organizing Model of Unionism, and no matter how sweetly you present these changes, some officers and members—and certainly your boss—will find any changes definitely unpleasant. For some officers, anything you do is a threat. They do not like it, and therefore they do not like you either. Get used to it and work around this problem by reaching out to the members who supported you in the first place.

One important thing to remember, however, is to avoid long-running and public personal disagreements with other officers, ex-officers and members. Your members did not vote for you to watch a petty and demeaning spectacle at every meeting over some obscure issue or over your bruised personal feelings. You need to focus on moving the union ahead and, if you do, these disagreements will fade away; people will not necessarily stop opposing you but you are at least facing toward the future and eventually you will get the support you need from the membership.

It is also important to see if you *really* disagree over a particular strategy. Often, a bunch of officers all want the same thing—like a new contract—but have very different ideas of how to get it done. It's like a group of friends who want to go to the same restaurant but each one has a different route to get there. Same thing in a local—you have a common goal but different ways to get there so there is only a question of strategy.

•***Personal Behavior***—In many ways, you will have to go through a major personality change as you become a new officer. Many jobs don't require interpersonal skills to be successful but being a union officer is about people. One union officer illustrated how difficult it sometimes is to make this change. He said "I had a guy come up to me with a question, but I never liked the guy and never wanted to have anything to do with him. So, I just ignored him."

Bad Union Practice.

As a member, you could pick and choose whom you associated with but now you are an officer, you represent ALL of your co-workers (even the non-members) so you better show them the respect of listening to them and trying to understand their problem.

The First Commandment for every union member is "Thou shall not bring discredit on the Union" and this is especially true for officers, who are the public face of our movement. How you speak, how you dress, what kind of car you drive and where you hang out in your off time may not be big issues for a member but when you become an officer, you need to look at where you go and how you act because you are now a public figure. In one building trades local, as an example, a member had a reputation for hanging out in bars and getting into scraps. While these fracases could be considered "a guy thing" when he was a member, once he was elected to office—and continued this behavior—he became a real liability for the local (and it may have been a factor when his slate was voted out in the next election).

Do you have a Facebook page or a Twitter account? Be very careful what you put up because it is all public. In fact, you will soon be dealing with grievances over members who post opinions—like the major league umpire who said that he would buy a weapon "because if you impeach MY PRESIDENT this way, YOU WILL HAVE ANOTHER CIVAL WAR!!!" or the UAW members who were fired after the 2019 GM strike for posting ""General Motors is sneaking in scabs to run the body shop. Need all people (out) there to stop them. Bring your ball bats, numb chicks (sic) and night sticks. It's time to step this up. It's time to get some national headlines coverage and turn the tables on Mary Barra. Be there and bring a friend."

And be careful about what you read. Here is a great discussion about "fake news" from Tim Sheard, originally published by Metro New York Labor Communications:

HOW TO IDENTIFY THAT INFORMATION IS FAKE

1.   Be skeptical of inflammatory, provocative images, videos & text: look at the stated source and, if you are not sure, verify it.

2.   Examine the web site's URL (web address) that provided the content. Often a rogue sender will use a source name that is similar enough to a legitimate one to fool you at first glance, like NYTomes.com for NY Times.com. Likewise, if the URL does not end in a .com, an .org or a .net, it may be from an untrustworthy source. Check it carefully.

3.   For a Facebook post, click on the name of the sender and check to see if it's a real, living person or if it's a fake account::

a. Photos: if you don't see a trove of photos on the sender's FB page of the individual, family, pets, vacations, etc., but only see stock photos of scenes, covers of books, etc., delete it and report it to FB as suspicious.

b. Short timeline: if you don't see a timeline with lots of events featuring the sender over a long period of time, with real people in the background, don't trust it.

c. Shared friends: chances are the sender should have a lot of friends in common with you. If they don't, look over their page carefully.

d. Impersonating a friend's FB page: Some hackers send you a friend request from someone you do know, but it is a scam. Click on the "friend's" name and check his/her FB page. If it doesn't look real, delete the request and report it.

e. Bottom line: report the bad actor to FB or Twitter or whatever the platform is so they can investigate and take it down.

As you look at the functions of the local in Chapter 5, by the way, you will find that social media is becoming a more important part of your grievance log—members posting things about your employer on their personal sites. If members post critical comments, they may be disciplined, and you will have the contentious debate about Freedom of Speech vs management policies. In some cases, unfortunately, a member may post a derogatory or threatening remark about a co-worker and, as an officer, you will not only have to deal with potential discipline from management, but opposition from your members who may not want the person in their workplace any longer

Now Go Do It!

TASKS:

1) Write it on an index card, and

2) Add one sentence describing how you can carry out each point.

4 UNDERTAKING STRATEGIC PLANNING

"The definition of insanity is doing something which doesn't work out, and then doing the same thing over and over again, and expecting the results to be different." — Rita Mae Brown

One important place to change your union is by supporting strategic planning, an element generally missing from most local unions.

In your personal life, you do strategic planning all of the time. Maybe it's buying a house or a new truck, or getting married, or divorced; or it's something as simple as figuring out where you are going on vacation or what education you need to change jobs. So, you go through a process of strategic planning, calculating where you want to go, how long you want to take, maybe how much it will cost or what education you have to obtain.

The same process applies to your local, although it is more complicated now because you have to organize your co-workers to agree on your strategic plan. Strategic planning requires a particular attitude so, as your boss often says, let's talk about an attitude adjustment!

Strategic planning reflects a *proactive* attitude! We have used this word proactive over and over again, as one of the most important characteristics of a good union officer at any level. Proactive means actively pushing for change, being aggressive, taking initiatives—and some risks—to build and expand the union. If you look at *Appendix 2*, for union leadership in The Organizing Model of Unionism, being proactive is included.

Being proactive is so important that one of your tasks is to chart all of your activities during a normal week (if there is such a thing as "normal" in the union) and have, as described in Chapter 2,the two To Do pads—one marked "Reactive,"—that is, issues started by the boss that you have to respond to—and "Proactive"—campaigns you want to start, issues you want to make a fight on.

Yes, we often have to fight reactive struggles because our bosses are always on the move. Management is taught in both the private and the public sectors that an employer that is not proactive is an employer that is about to go out of business. So, the bosses are constantly messing with us: introducing new technology, new work practices, opening new facilities (sometimes halfway around the world) or threatening to subcontract some of our work. In every case, the union must take up the challenge. In every reactive event, however, the boss makes the first move and picks the issues that we will fight about, hoping that we will fight more with each other than with the boss.

In most unions, many officers plan strategically only as far as their next election. How can you change this? As part of a proactive approach, you need to create a program, finding issues that are either promising (they look like hot topics) or necessary (there is a new contract coming up) that will increase membership participation. Look ahead a month, six months, a year to try to anticipate what challenges you will have. The union needs to pick the issues, even if it means rousing the membership to take on a problem that they have battled and maybe even lost in the past. Strategic planning fits into the whole structure for renewing and rebuilding your local union. After all, isn't that why you ran for office in the first place?

Many employers spent a lot of time and money on issues like strategic planning and decision-making, loading up employees with mumbo-jumbo about left brain, right brain and active listening. In most cases, we ignore these exercises because it is proven that the boss will simply go ahead and do what he thinks is best—right or wrong—no matter what the workers feel. These techniques can work, however, if you use them inside your local, so it won't hurt to pay a little more attention the next time the boss runs a workshop.

Another area that will cause you great problems is making decisions, specifically making *new* decisions. In many unions, all decisions seem routine because the officers are simply following the well-worn trail laid out by Old Joe over the years. This approach is no longer possible or desirable, as the declining membership numbers demonstrate. Unions are at the center of a dramatically changing universe, so even if we wanted to keep on keeping on, outside forces make it impossible. Companies are started up, bought, sold, expanded, contracted, taken global, taken into bankruptcy; public agencies "reinvent" themselves with leaner and meaner policies. New technology changes the way our work is performed and how our industries function.

There is no more "normal," so Old Joe has been left behind. As an officer, you will have to create a new method for making these new decisions. You will have to build an organization to present various alternatives, and their consequences, always stretching to get your membership involved at every step.

Your ability to make changes and to organize your co-workers around important decisions will generally depend on how you handle *The Network*. Every organization has The Network—a small group of members who have controlled decisions and elections for a long time. In a union, it is not uncommon for The Network to be comprised of good ol' boys, but a network can be made up of good ol' gals as well. The point is that, in a union, these members have been in office and have controlled who is in office for a long time.

It is ironic that modern unionism, which hopes to bring some sort of democracy to the workplace, is internally a totalitarian, or one-party, organization, whether it is at the lowest shop level or at the highest ranks of the international union. It neither appreciates nor encourages opposition and looks upon dissenting views or new officers like you as an obstacle to be overcome, and not as an improvement on a status quo.

As a new officer, you either ran as a choice of The Network, or you ran as an outsider, against the flow. Either way, if you see the urgency of protecting your union, and unionism in general, then some of these points will be helpful.

As a newcomer, you should be prepared to do things in a completely different way. In a traditional local, as you saw in the chart on The Servicing Model of Unionism [*Appendix 1*], the leadership makes all of the important decisions and simply offers the membership an occasional chance to rubber-stamp the decisions. Often these decisions are only communicated to the membership in a half-hearted way, if at all. When decisions for the union are made by one person, or a small group, with no participation by the members, the small group often will claim more knowledge or experience, or will warn that any discussion will show the union is divided. As a result, most of the members come to work under their union contract without a clue about what the union is doing. The larger the union, or the broader the contract, the less membership involvement there is. The Network has run the local for years and likes it that way even if the world is going to hell.

These officers have perfected the skills of staying in office, so any changes only threaten the stability that they desire. They will constantly try to frustrate your attempts to change the way the union operates and will even go behind your back to try to discredit you in front of the members. A new officer can spend a lot of time and go through a lot of aggravation trying to change an executive board, for example, and neglect the membership that put him/her in office.

Does this mean that all existing officers are totally useless? Not at all. In fact, you should evaluate each one to see if you can get some of them headed in the direction of greater membership involvement. Just don't be surprised or disappointed if they won't back you up.

How can you set up a method for building a new direction for your local? By developing what we will call a *program*, or **Action Plan**, for dealing with issues of importance and for increasing membership involvement. Everything you do should be directed to increasing membership involvement, a practice that many long-time officers find scary. You were elected, however, by a membership that was not happy with the direction of the union, who wanted change and focus. You will be letting them down if you simply lapse into the ways of the old organization.

As a target, set a goal of having every member of your union involved in at least two union activities during the next year. It doesn't have to be as an officer—it can be signing on to a group grievance, it can be participating in a union social activity, it can be spending time on an organizing or political campaign. In short, ANYTHING—just as long as it's a union activity.

One important component of this strategic planning is signing up your non-members if you are in an open shop state so,as you set up an Action Plan, one element must be: will this help us sign up non-members? With all of the anti-union attacks, and negative court decisions about union security, increasing your membership is crucial. And what better time to approach these free riders than when the union is being overhauled? You may find that some of them have old complaints about the officers. These officers are gone, so there's now no excuse not to join the union.

To find out what issues your members want the union to confront, you could do a survey, asking what changes your members want to see in their workplace and in the union. Just conducting the survey will mean talking with—and listening to—your members. There is one "survey" that you already took, however. When you ran for office and campaigned around your workplace, you heard loud and clear what problems your members had about how their union was being run. This was your first "listening tour," and your members voted for you because they wanted change. You may have committed yourself to some of the changes as part of your campaign but the very fact that you have a plan sets you apart from the large majority of union members.

The elements of a strategic plan are pretty simple. The action itself is the difficult part so your campaign needs an *Action Plan* that can be shared with all of your members. The easiest way to develop this plan is to list the goal(s) you want to achieve and then figure out what it will take to accomplish them, how long it should take and how much it will cost. It is helpful to make large written charts and post them on a wall. The goals may be easy, like having an outing to get the families of your members involved in the union, or difficult, like winning a new contract or dealing with a threatened plant closing.

List Goals

Revise the Plan   **ACTION**

PLAN   Assemble
Resources

Estimate Timeframe
& budget

If you are looking for an issue to use to evaluate any officers, their positions on increasing membership involvement is the best one. Make your case that increasing membership involvement is the most critical task the local union faces. Evaluate every decision as the answer to this question: will it get more members, and their families, and the community, involved in the struggles of this local union?

The method for planning a campaign is simple to understand and often difficult to accomplish. It is an essential component of strategic planning and it looks like this:

- Describe the problem.

- Prepare for the campaign in a positive way. Too many union officers hope a plan fails so that they can gain a political advantage by blaming another officer.

- Set a goal for resolving the problem. Be as bold and ambitious as possible.

- Collect any necessary information that is related to the problem.

- Create a full discussion—often called brainstorming—to get a sense of the different ideas for reaching your goal. Many heads are better than one, right? Build in as many members as possible and make sure that it is discussed thoroughly so that, if the plan fails, everyone will share the responsibility and you won't be a target.

- Summarize the decision in writing, including a specific assignment of responsibilities, so that everyone can agree on who is supposed to do what and when. Accountability is very important.

- Create a time line and set specific points to evaluate the process and your decisions as you go along. You may want to break up your campaign into specific stages, checking each one as you go along.

- Build into the plan any financial considerations for the local. What expenses could be involved? Is the activity worth the members' dues money?

- Build in a "nag factor"—that is, who will have the responsibility for keeping on everyone to make sure they are doing what they agreed to do. It is very important that everyone involved in this decision buy into the plan, and that they agree to do certain things, rather than having them arbitrarily assigned by The Network.

While it is a great help to have a written Action Plan for every activity so you know exactly what you are going to do and who is going to do it, one reader of this book stressed that knowing how to develop a budget is an essential part of any change. As an officer, you now have control and responsibility for the union's money. The responsibility for both shrewdly using these resources and being able to account to your members is crucial. Bad enough that a campaign flops: you don't want to also be accused of throwing away the members' money.

So, pick a project and try out this model of strategic planning. The project may be simple, like cleaning up the union hall or holding the family outing, or it may be difficult, like finishing up all of the old grievances, winning a new contract or organizing some non-union workers in another location. As a rule, it is better to start with an easier project, so that everyone can become accustomed to the new way of doing things and so that there is a good chance you will be successful. Success in a small project always makes people more willing to take on a big one. In any case, simply follow the format of a strategic plan and keep working on it.

You may visualize yourself as a scoutmaster leading hundreds of kids on an outing: when you move, you have to move hundreds of them as well, an effort that may remind you of the expression "herding cats." Officers sometimes make decisions based on their own situations and don't pause to consider whether the rest of the troop can move as fast or understands as much as they do. Remember that leadership is not what you do, but what you get others to do.

As new decisions have to be made, even the smallest issue will seem controversial. Many new officers are paralyzed after being elected because issues have so many vocal proponents on either side. Simple administrative issues become controversial, and a new officer often tries to retreat into the safe area of "I don't know what to do," as if this were an option.

One important consideration in your strategic planning is how many other officers are willing to help you, and how many of them who opposed your campaign will try to block you and embarrass you. After every election, you can calculate the power you have among your officers—see if you can persuade some of the old officers that the union needs a new direction, or else start looking ahead to the next election when you can recruit some new candidates. One of the worst situations is when a local is paralyzed because of disagreement among the officers—not disagreement over important issues, but quarrels over petty politics and self-interest. Incumbent officers can be intimidating, especially if new officers forget how they got elected: new forces in your union showed up to vote for a change and put you into office. Don't be hesitant about going back to them for support. Chapter 6, on Communications, will give you some ways to do this.

The most important things to remember are:
- You gotta have a plan, or program. Know where you want the union to go and avoid being dragged along or forced to suffer because of external pressures.
- Know the meaning of the word *proactive.*
- You *always* must have an element of membership involvement attached to *every* part of your program, as well as a focus on signing up non-members if you have some.
- Figure out a way to go around other local leadership, directly to the members if you have to.
- Don't get discouraged or disorganized, because you'll defeat yourself.
- Ask questions. While this may seem ridiculously obvious, it may be the first priority for a new officer. Depending on your experience in the union, you may know a lot or you may know nothing, but you must decide to make it a priority to learn as much as possible as fast as possible.It will astound you (OK, maybe you expect it) how defensive old officers get when someone asks them to explain why they do what they do. Remember that your membership elected you to be a leader, so you have to know what's going on.

Now Go Do It!

TASKS:

1) Evaluate each of the other officers in terms of willingness to change, on a scale of 1 (already changing) to 10 (wouldn't change without dynamite).

2) Do a chart of all of the issues you handle for the union, and mark each one P (for proactive) or R (for reactive). Then look at how you are spending your time, as a kind of pattern.

3) Pick a project for the local to undertake and see if you can get some of the other officers and members to create a strategic plan.

4) Once the project is completed, evaluate this first strategic effort to see where you were successful and where you need to make some adjustments in future efforts.

5 ANALYZING THE FUNCTIONS OF THE UNION

Once you are elected, you will find out a great many new things, and not all of them will be pleasant. Often, any information passed along to the members by the previous union officers had a self-serving element involved: make the officers look good, avoid open discussions of troublesome situations and create a structure that prevents the membership from interfering in decision-making that the officers have taken on for themselves. Even if your election as an officer was supported by the other officers—you succeeded an officer who retired or died, for example—you are still faced with the challenge of an organization in decline, as the numbers in Appendix 3 demonstrate.

You also need to recognize that, as a member, or steward, you saw only pieces and bits of the whole functioning of your union. If you were a steward, you knew the work, the issues and the personalities of your department. As an officer, you have to know the whole workplace. As a member of the negotiating committee, you sat back and watched someone else make decisions. Now it's your turn.

You have to take a crash course in *all* the functions of your union. This chapter is simply a very brief introduction because each element of the local union could be covered in a full book. Don't be overwhelmed by all that you have to learn or by the difficulties you may have in getting specific information about some of these functions—about how they are carried out or, just as important, why no one is doing them. There is often specialized training available for new officers and you should consider sharpening your skills as quickly as possible.

It is helpful to make a list of all of the functions of your union so you can begin to see how the various parts work and so you and your co-workers can decide how to set things straight. You will often find some confusion over what is being done and what ought to be done. Areas like new organizing and political action, for example, which are both expensive and controversial, are often ignored at the local level or passed off to another layer of the union, like a District or a Council of the International Union.

An initial task is to clearly define the responsibilities—and accountability—of each officer, especially in areas like grievances, contract negotiations, communications and overall strategy. It is also critical, as will be discussed in Chapter 6, to establish financial oversight—you may know who signs the checks, but who evaluates each invoice? As you look at the various functions of the local, your best plan is to make a list with the categories *Who Does?* and *Who Pays?* After all, the control of resources is an essential part of union strategy and now you, as a new officer, have to participate in these decisions.

Many officers will deny that some functions truly are the responsibility of the union at their level. They are particularly sensitive to the question of *Who Pays* since most officers don't want to spend "their" money on some activities,

such as organizing, that they really don't want to do. By claiming that some other level of the union is responsible for an activity like new organizing, the result is that lots of great speeches are made, lots of fingers are pointed, and nothing gets done and our membership sits at 1900 levels. As we have repeatedly stated, of course, if unionism were successful and growing, then the model could continue. The movement is declining, so it is change or die. Pointing fingers and playing a blame game will not reverse the decline.

It is essential that you and the other officers have a clear sense of these relationships between the different levels of your union—your local, the district or joint council, and the International Union. There have been, unfortunately, issues of pressure or direct interference in local issues by representatives of these other levels. It is obviously critical that representatives from every level of the union agree on strategy and procedures and, as a new officer, you need to make this happen because it is the local officers who have to face members who are disgruntled over decisions that are out of the control of local officers.

It is important at this point to not be intimidated—yes, many of the reps for the District or the International have years of experience, but their interests may not be the same as yours or your local's. And let's not forget that their track record—based on the decline in union membership and on prevalent contract concessions—is not one of wild success.

危机

CRISIS AS OPPORTUNITY
(wēi jī)

The Chinese word for "crisis" is made up of two parts: "danger" and "opportunity".

危

"Danger", originally pictured as a man on the edge of a precipice

机

"Opportunity"—a reminder of the seemingly small but important opportunity that can come out of danger.

Your International rep may not be the best resource for all of your local's needs. One new officer remarked that he found that the International reps were "not much help with major issues like health care and pensions so we had to develop our own members as in-house experts" in order to quickly respond to the crisis of the 2007-2009 recession.

One way for you, as a new officer, to resolve the debate over which level of the union is responsible for these basic functions is to agree that *all* levels of the union are responsible. Since you are an officer at the local level, you'd better start where you are, always good advice in any organizing situation. It was all well and good to go to various union functions and blast away at other officers for their failings. Now you are an officer (we have met the enemy and they are us!) so it is your responsibility and your opportunity to move your union in a different direction.

It is also important to look at all of these functions of the union as an opportunity, not as a headache. The Chinese character for "crisis" combines both "danger" and "opportunity." The more activities the union carries out, the more opportunity for more members to participate in areas that interest them.

Have you noticed that all of your existing local union committees are filled by the same-old same-old—a small group of union regulars who seem to do everything? You should immediately reach out and recruit new members. Be *proactive* in your organizing and don't simply announce a new committee and hope that someone new will miraculously show up. Expanded membership involvement should also be targeted to increasing the diversity of your leadership—seniority, race, gender, sexual orientation, geography, skill level, language.

One important organizing principle is to ask a new participant to carry out a very specific task with a limited time investment. A big problem with internal organizing is approaching your co-workers with the open-ended plea to "get involved." Better to ask a person to perform one very specific task with a beginning and an end and in a limited time span, so your members can get used to participation a little at a time. It is also important, as every organizer knows, to assign a task that the member can successfully accomplish: nothing succeeds like success, after all, so evaluate the talents of your members and be flexible. Just like a coach who figures out the best position for a player to be successful, you need to put your members where they will enjoy their assignments and will be great. A member who does well on one task, gets the satisfaction of finishing it and is showered with plenty of "attaboys" or "attagirls" is a prime prospect to return for more.

Let's look at the list and see how your union handles its responsibilities, recognizing that many of the union's basic functions—like grievances, negotiations and organizing—are whole subjects in themselves and can only be briefly covered here.

1) Grievances. The enforcement of the contract has always been one of the basic functions of a workers' organization, even before there were unions as we know them today. It is also an area where most of the members are in the dark, unless one has an individual grievance. This ignorance is a major waste because using grievances to build the union has been a proven success. Workplace issues—if properly developed—can weave the members into the activity of the union through group grievances and workplace solidarity activities.

The discussion of grievance strategy—and even whether you *have* a grievance strategy!—is a long topic. At the beginning, though, you should become familiar with the process used by both the union and the boss for resolving the daily problems and frictions that are the nature of any workplace. If you have come up through the steward system, you already have some of this knowledge but now you will become familiar with other departments or shifts.

Under The Servicing Model of Unionism, grievances are handled almost in secrecy by a small group of officers and stewards. It is a good guess that no more than 5% of all members are affected by a grievance in any particular year—if you haven't been fired or been denied a job bid or seen your work subcontracted, you have no contact with the grievance procedure. Maybe the officers make a report at the local meeting on grievances they considered important, and maybe they don't bother. Maybe a grievance gets discussed because an unhappy member shows up to bitch—loudly and repeatedly—about how an individual grievance was handled. Maybe members who turn out for a meeting never return because so much time was wasted arguing over individual grievances.

Many good officers and stewards will argue that members don't know enough about the contract or about how to manipulate a grievance, so they should not wander into an area where they might cause damage. You need to understand, however, that every officer and steward came new into your workplace neither knowing the grievance procedure nor understanding anything about presenting one. They learned, and the rest of your members can too.

In any case, the grievance procedure has not expanded membership participation. You need to think about grievances, then, as part of your organizing campaign, in which you want to involve as many members as possible in particular issues. By becoming proactive, you can find issues that excite the membership rather than simply reacting to something the boss has done.

Look at grievances, then, in a new way—as a way to do more than enforce your contract. Look at them as a way to *build your union* and to involve your membership and you will be off to a great start as a new officer. You will also begin to understand *leverage*—the ability to make your boss do what he doesn't want to do.

So how does your local handle grievances?

- Do individual stewards or committee people have sole authority to go forward with a worker's complaint, or does a member get to appeal to you as an officer? Who has the final authority on investigating and/or filing a written grievance?

- Are there guidelines for filing grievances or is it a haphazard process? Do stewards have to fill out a "Fact Sheet" before filing a grievance?

- How does your union track grievances—that is, record which complaints are registered by a member, which disputes are "settled," which complaints are officially filed as written grievances, which ones are carried forward?

- More important—and here is an area where most unions are horribly backward—how do your members know in general what is going on with their grievances? Do you publicize all grievance activity? If you don't, you should, so that members (and, obviously, the non-members whom you want to sign up) appreciate that the union is an active force all of the time, and not just during contract negotiations.

- At the very least, is there an individual "report-back," from a steward to a member with a problem, so the member knows what is going on with a complaint?

Look at *organizing campaigns* in the workplace to support grievances as a way to get your membership involved—and to sign up non-members. Expanding simple grievances into group grievances signed by many workers, even if you don't need the signatures to process the grievance, is an example of a proactive approach, especially when supported by workplace activities, and gives new expression to long-running battles. Expand your definition of "bargaining"—often we get into a rut and accept management's definition of their rights so that there are many issues of concern that are declared "not bargainable," or off-limits. Remember that your contract's recognition clause [*Appendix 7*] gives the union the right to negotiate over wages, hours and terms and conditions of employment—and this is *everything*! Even off-duty conduct—like social media or personal behavior—can be issues for discipline and are therefore open for bargaining. Expand your vision and you will be able to initiate a lot of good causes.

Any strategy is only as good as the people who carry it out, so carefully evaluate your steward system. Do you have a steward for every department and every shift? Under your bylaws, are they elected or appointed? And most importantly, are they capable and bold? So much of successful grievance handling is the steward, so be sure to get good ones and to train them well. One of the biggest failures of union leadership is the assumption that being a steward is not a special skill, that anyone with a good heart or political loyalty should be able to do it. Not true. As employers become more aggressive, it is essential to train—and retrain—all of your stewards. It is an investment that will pay dividends many times over.

As part of your local strategic planning you should create, or revive, a stewards' council that meets regularly to discuss pending grievances or workplace problems and that can become an educational circle for all of your stewards and officers. This council should also become an area for education, training and recruitment of potential new stewards. The exchange of Best Union Practices among stewards of different locations, and different unions, is very important.

2) Negotiations. For many members, the union is only a live wire during the collective bargaining season, the period when a new contract is being negotiated. At this time, on their own, members suddenly develop a big interest in what the union is doing. Attendance at meetings increases, special meetings and activities are going on and there is either profound excitement or profound depression—depending on the progress of negotiations—throughout the workplace. In many union elections over the past few years, at every level, a lousy contract was the trigger that started an insurgent movement: you may have campaigned against such a contract. Here is an area where you can make your mark as a new officer, especially if you start planning for negotiations that may be some months in the future.

KEEP
CALM
AND
PROVIDE
LEVERAGE

As a new officer, you may get to participate in these negotiations as a member of the committee or at least you are supposed to be more involved than you were as a rank-and-file member. You will also become familiar with the concept of "leverage"—developing enough power in the union to make the boss do what he doesn't want to do. Negotiations used to be easy back when employers wanted to reach an agreement and were not contaminated with anti-unionism. The union committee would show up and have heated debates with management and then there would be a settlement, or occasionally a strike. The world of unionism is today a very different place and nowhere does this become more obvious than in negotiations so learn the slogan "Get Leverage or Go Home" and spread it to your members.

In the past, knowing your employer was easy and helped you to figure out leverage—you could strike or slow-down one location, or one corporation and get what you wanted. New patterns of ownership—global capital, private and shadowy equity firms with PO boxes in the Cayman Islands—show the importance of research before you even sit down at the table. Who's the Boss and how can you squeeze him?

There is now a kind of romantic version of going on strike, as if it's the only way a union can be tough. Once again, in your planning for negotiations, look for leverage—if a strike works, fine, but there can be many other ways to squeeze your employer and make the union strong.

It is unfortunate how many unions use total secrecy as a negotiating "strategy." Reflecting another essential component of The Servicing Model of Unionism, the officers believe that the members are not smart enough to follow the bargaining's twists and turns, proposals and counterproposals. Negotiations are carried out under a blackout policy, a strategy often suggested by your boss as a way to "move negotiations along!" When the boss suggests something to "improve" negotiations, put your hand on your wallet and keep it there. In fact, the suggestions by the boss to move negotiations along are usually the opposite of the way to build the union. As a result, the negotiations go poorly for the union.

Negotiations should be used as a way to keep up your members' interest in the union. Tell them everything; make them participate in all decisions. Even consider "open bargaining," so members can sit in with the negotiating committee and see first-hand what you are up against. Create a website, use an e-mail list, and leaflet your workplace. Your union will be much stronger for it, and you will be a better officer. After all, one of your main campaign planks was improved communications among the members, wasn't it? What better place to carry this out than in contract negotiations?

Another effective strategy suggested by some new officers is the pre-negotiations bargaining survey, which is passed out to every member (and maybe even to non-members in an open shop as an incentive for them to join) so the contract becomes the topic of discussion throughout the workplace and everyone feels involved. Even if your workplace is so small that everyone knows everyone else, pass out a survey anyway as a way to increase the sense of participation.

It is also essential to understand the principle of *bargaining between contracts* (or *continuous bargaining*), which puts your union in the proactive position of trying constantly to win improvements in the workplace, using the negotiations as a method for continuing and expanding membership involvement. In The Servicing Model of Unionism, the ratification of a new contract usually means that the leadership of the union slides back into its old routines. Your boss, however, is not quite so careless. The ink is barely dry on the new contract before he is trying to change conditions and to chisel away at improvements you thought the union had locked up. The union is then forced to fight a series of rear-guard and defensive actions, usually without a sense of organization or initiative. The boss is bargaining between contracts, right?

What if the union took the same approach—that we need to be constantly after improvements in our working conditions? Smart leaders use proactive grievances to continually force the boss to negotiate over issues in the workplace. These leaders find that the membership's sense of involvement and excitement is the same as during "regular" negotiations. Look at situations that were not resolved in negotiations and try to figure out how you can reopen the issue—as a grievance, as a demand to bargain over a change in conditions, as a popular movement in the workplace. All of the attention that members give to union activities in contract negotiations will be revived as you bargain between contracts.

3) New Organizing. While this activity is not recognized by most local unions, it is, or should be, one of the essential functions of an active membership because organizing your employer's competitors, or non-union facilities, will bring you leverage in negotiations and grievances, directly benefitting your members (and helping your chances for re-election). The lack of any sense of organizing, by the way, is a strong symptom of the disconnect between the top levels of union leadership, who are finally talking about organizing, and the membership, who have not heard even a whisper about the importance of expanding our union movement. Creating a "culture of organizing," is essential so that your members understand that a decline in members, or a decline in percent-age of unionized workers, at your employer and in the world as a whole, is a direct and dangerous threat to their wages and working conditions. How often do we see today the closing of old facilities so that work can be consolidated—in a non-union location? Don't wait for the stroke of doom—start organizing now. Set up a committee of volunteer organizers, who will first focus the membership on the importance of new organizing, then scout out the landscape for desirable local targets and help an organizer build campaigns there. For a more thorough discussion of organizing, look at *From First Contact to First Contract: A Union Organizer's Handbook.*

It is also important to learn organizing skills because the same methods that your "professional" organizers should use on new organizing can also be directly applied to expanding your membership involvement, or internal organizing. Once again, just because a worker pays union dues does not mean that he or she is truly a union *member*. A comprehensive organizing program overlaps all of the union's activities, and you should keep this at the front of your strategic planning.

If you are operating in an open shop state (also mistakenly known as a "right-to-work" state), new organizing also includes *internal* organizing: getting workers in your bargaining unit who are not members—the free riders—to join up. Increasing your membership will build both your bargaining power and your financial status. Looking at grievances or negotiations, for example, as opportunities to sign up new members should always be part of your strategy. This whole topic of signing up new members is the focus of another book, *Closing Up the Open Shop: A Guide to Internal Organizing.*

4) Political Action. Politics is important—to our members, and especially to public-sector workers, and to non-union workers who traditionally have depended upon union strength to raise conditions for all of us. But the political action committee has been a dead zone of the local union, another example of the failure of The Servicing Model of Unionism. As you can see on the chart on Political Action [*Appendix 4*], The Servicing Model basically expects the membership to rise up on cue at the direction of the leadership for some clearly defined functions(poll watching, phone banking, etc.) but otherwise to exert no power on the so-called political activities of the union officers, which are usually restricted to following around whatever Democrat is in, or running for, office.

THE PEOPLE DON'T KNOW THEIR TRUE POWER.

It is clear from the legislation passed—or not—at all levels that unionism's political influence has been feeble and needs a whole new game plan. One important lesson from the election of Donald Trump in 2016 is that union members have minds, and opinions, of their own which are usually dismissed. Even though the official union PACs and officers strongly supported Hillary Clinton, about 46% of our members voted for Trump, about the same number that voted in 1984 for Ronald Reagan, after he destroyed PATCO, the union of air traffic controllers.

In far too many states, candidates have run strong anti-union campaigns, making unions the villains and blaming us for everything from budget deficits to poor schools to traffic delays and potholes.

There are glimpses of change, however. One powerful example was in the 2019 elections in Virginia, where a huge shift to the Democrats was seen and, immediately after the election, union officers convened a meeting to discuss repeal of the state's Open Shop/Right-to-Work law, an enormously important and ambitious demand. In response, Governor Ralph Northam promptly responded, "I can't foresee Virginia taking actions [that would include] repeal of the right-to-work law," to which one union member ruefully responded: "and we knocked on doors for this guy?"

At the same time, in small towns, like Lorain, Ohio, or in large cities like Seattle, union members have broken from the usual allegiance to Democrats and have run themselves to defend unionism and to protect non-union workers.As a new officer, elected to revitalize the union, you need to look at these movements to see how they could work in your area. And in every campaign, you need to make unionism a fundamental issue, with specific demands that a candidate has to support in order to get union backing.

Many union officers use the political diversity of the membership as an excuse not to bring the membership into political activity. After all, the argument goes, the workers are too diverse to *really* understand politics or get distracted by "social" issues, like religion, abortion or gun control. The argument is made to focus on "bread-and-butter" issues and leave the more divisive social issues out, even though most political campaigns now revolve around these issues. All disagreements are best debated openly, even if the discussions are often drawn-out and sometimes very hot.

This approach creates huge and often unresolved issues among the members who do not agree with the political positions of the leaders and spend time muttering in the workplace about the failure of the union. In fact, the issue that Mark Janus grabbed as the basis for his lawsuit against Fair Share requirements was the union's donation to Planned Parenthood.

One same argument is used in every area of the union to support The Servicing Model of Unionism: the members are too dumb and should not be drawn in over their heads. If you believe this, as a new officer, then you are no better than the officer you replaced.

Trust your membership to learn.

You did, didn't you?

After all, the members were smart enough to elect you.

5) Hiring Hall. While most unions do not control hiring, many building trades or entertainment industry unions do assign work, and patterns of favoritism can be a factor in local union elections, especially when work is slow. Discontent about work assignments among desperate members is always a campaign issue, so a new officer needs to set up a strict policy so members are treated fairly and procedures are clearly defined for everyone. As you will see in Chapter 8, officers of a union can be legally responsible for bad practices at the hiring hall and may expose the union to financial penalties.

6) Local union meetings. It may seem odd to describe your regular, or special, meetings as a function of the union but here is where your members gather and where a difference between the two models of unionism can be dramatically seen.In the Servicing Model, officers discourage members from attending—even while some union constitutions prevent members from running for office if they miss too many meetings. As one new local union officer put it, "A new officer needs to change the attitude of how a meeting is run from a dictator[ship] to an open kind of discussion." If there can be a frank and candid exchange of opinions at the meeting—presented soberly and respectfully, of course—members will be encouraged to return.

It was a rare event when IBEW Local 1250 in Rapid City, SD, hired two labor educators, John Lund and Don Taylor, to survey their members to answer a crucial question: why don't more members attend union meetings? The answers were widely scattered in a local that has multiple workplaces, but issues of scheduling and locations were important topics.

If the officers you ran against were concerned about your local, they would have carried out a similar program, right? So now you can do the survey. Just setting it up signals to your members that their participation is so important.

An officer can also survey the members to see what special activities or guest speakers would be a draw, and then schedule accordingly. Simply getting your members to fill out such a survey is a form of membership involvement and, in my experience, they are startled, and pleased, to be asked. One new officer suggested that, at every meeting, old members be encouraged to give a short history of the local, or relate past events so that younger members will begin to understand that all of the union benefits they enjoy came from struggles in the past and were not simply handed out by a benevolent boss.

7) Social activities. Back in the day, local unions had all kinds of activities: softball teams, bowling leagues, cook-outs, amateur theatricals, even fashion shows. Since most workers lived near their workplaces, there was an almost unbroken road from the workplace to community or recreational activities. Local officers sponsored anything that would get members, their families, their retirees and the community together.

Numerous factors over the past 25 years have dramatically decreased the role of the local union as a center for workers' lives. Prosperity, the interstate highway system, the internet and cable, changes in the old neighborhoods—all have dispersed your members, making it more difficult to get them back to the union hall for anything but the most basic activities.

Try anyway!

Most locals cannot reach a proper balance on social activities and either have too few or too many. There is no question that social activities, especially those that "expand" your local by inviting family members, friends, retirees and community residents into your circle of activities, are very important in building your union. Social occasions also allow a great entry for new members and offer a sense of engagement, especially since these activities are "non-threatening."

Consider non-threatening activities as you approach your co-workers to encourage them to get involved in union events. They will carefully weigh the risks and the possible rewards of each activity. Every member knows from tough experience exactly how far your boss will go in allowing union activities. In some cases, a vindictive boss will punish active union officers for their union involvement by moving them to a lousy shift or a crummy job. All of your co-workers have witnessed these activities, and may not be willing to jump immediately from non-activity to the front line of the battle between the workers and the boss. So, some kinds of union activities can be seen as "threatening"—there can be negative consequences for positive union activity. A social activity, however, is relatively "non-threatening." After all, even the most rotten boss can hardly be against a retiree outing or a family holiday party. Can he?

Social occasions are a wonderful way to create a sense of solidarity and community among your members, families, retirees, other unions and the outside community. In public sector unions, where the taxpayers are the "employer," it is really important to bring the community into your local activities so that your neighbors can see that you are not greedy monsters but decent and hard-working people with the same goals and ambitions for yourselves and your families. The recent teacher strikes, which make broad social demands—like increased public housing—show how central our unions can be in our communities.

Social activities are especially important if the members of your union have not, so to speak, grown up together. In many unions under a national contract, new members transfer into your workplace from other facilities, bringing different work practices and experiences, often different languages and backgrounds. Knowing no one in their new town, their families either dragging along with them or remaining behind, such workers can make the union their family. At one UAW/GM plant the members of the shop held special welcoming parties and regular social events to welcome these transfers. At another UAW/GM facility, the transfers were made to feel like outcasts and strangers—hardly a way to build the union.

One local combined membership meetings with social activities, and found the best way to get second-shift workers to a meeting after work was to make it a kind of party, with food and beer. "These young guys were going out to party after work anyway, so why not get them to party with the union?" the local president said.

An important element of building up your local union is watching other organizations and how they grow. In many metropolitan areas, the mega-church has become common, and the ministers are very active in using social activities to draw new people and their families into church. The churches run constant activities—outings, clubs, affinity groups, family activities—and a local union could follow the example.

8) Cultural affairs. One way to make your union a center of attention is to encourage your members and families to express their lighter sides, by sponsoring different kinds of shows—art, music, theater, movies, anything that will make your union a center of activity. Sometimes these cultural activities can have a "union" theme, even though the participants are amateurs. One union, Hospital Workers Local 1199, started a cultural exhibit that grew over the years into the famous Bread and Roses Foundation which creates wonderful art exhibits, as well as music and theater productions that travel across the country. In the 1930's, the International Ladies Garment Workers Union (ILGWU), created the musical *Pins and Needles* and another, in 1954, supported the movie *Salt of the Earth*.

With the availability of new video techniques, it would be easy to make a history of the union, or record a discussion of an important topic, or even create your own musical. Your union does not have to be so ambitious, but creating a local union history, for example, which can hang at your union hall or be displayed in local schools, is a great way to both tap into the creative talents of your members and their families and to celebrate your union.

Maybe members could do a stream cleanup or spend a day with Habitat for Humanity. There is no shortage of good causes—and you can always go picket with another union—and these activities build so much solidarity, as members from different departments and background finally work together.

Have parties or shows that involve the children of your members; these shows will not only get more members involved in the union, but also will create a positive union education for the families—a necessary antidote for the anti-unionism that they are being taught in schools, thanks to an ambitious and well-funded effort by our bosses.

One union even started a movie night, showing movies like *Norma Rae* and *Matewan,* which are histories of the workers' movement and show the conflicts that surround individual workers when they get into a movement.

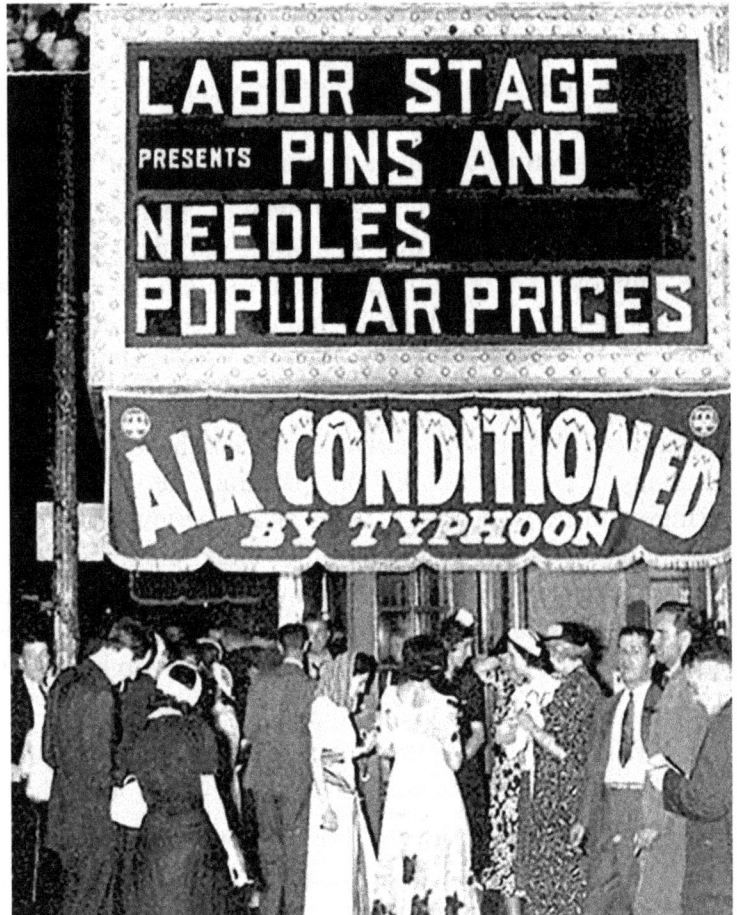

9) Benefit Funds. If your local is involved in health and welfare or pension funds, you should stick your nose into these areas to see how they operate. Because of the Taft-Hartley Act, there are no longer funds which are completely controlled by the union, even though they are called "union" funds. The bosses get to have an equal number of trustees, who run the fund along with the union trustees, but the union officers get the blame from their members when the funds fall short. This group usually hires specialists, either to invest the money in the fund or to administer payments. Usually, the union trustees are appointed by the officers of the union and operate pretty much in secret. So long as the benefits are available for the members, no one raises a stink.

As a result of both the Recession of 2007-2009 and a shifting of political pressure, these funds present a financial challenge to officers. Investment returns have dropped and many members now work fewer hours. With health and welfare funds gasping for income, some trustees have had to cut eligibility or benefits—not exactly a winning campaign issue in a local election. Politically, the move to eliminate defined benefit pensions is seeping over into union funds, with proposed reductions in benefits or even a shift to individual plans like 401(k)s or "cafeteria" plans. As wages are diverted to pay these costs, or as benefits are cut because of dwindling income, the benefit funds become a source of irritation and concern for members who otherwise pay no attention.

The discussion in December, 2019, about the Teamster Central States Pension Fund illustrates another potential hazard for a new officer. Due to decisions made in 2008-2009, the fund lost $11.1 billion—about 42% of its assets—so now the retirees are facing a 50% cut in benefits. The danger for a new officer is that decisions made years ago by officers who may now be long gone can come back to bite you in the you-know-where because you have to face your angry members to explain, or make excuses, for someone else's poor decisions.

In the public sector, pension funds have seen a disastrous drop, often due to the shrewd calculations of anti-union politicians and the lack of focus from union officers. In New Jersey, for example, governors and lawmakers for decades contributed less than the amount recommended by actuaries or nothing at all, so in 2018, the pension trust was underfunded by $130.7 billion—yeah, BILLION—and could cover only about 38.4% of projected retirement benefits for the projected 800,000 current and projected retirees. While New Jersey was the worst, across the country, state pension funds were only funded at a 72.5 % ratio. Union members take jobs in the public sector because of attractive retirement benefits and usually just assume that the money will be there—and it isn't. Even if an elected politician is not anti-union, spending tax moneys on gifts to developers seems more attractive than contributing to a pension fund, and then we face a crisis. As a new officer, learn how the fund operates and demand that payments be made, in full and on time.

Benefit funds also intensify existing splits in your membership: in discussing pensions, for example, the older workers want more money set aside for retirement benefits while younger workers prefer the money in wages. Bargaining benefit issues affects so many areas in the local that you better become familiar with all of the options and it is a great way to get all of your members involved, even the younger ones.

As an example globally, union workers have become much more militant about protecting retirement income. In early December, 2019, an estimated half-million workers struck in France to protest President Emmanuel Macron's plan to merge "France's complex of 42 different generous pension schemes into one state-managed system," as part of his campaign to reverse "a secure but sclerotic French system deemed too unfriendly to business, growth and job creation."

It is also helpful to remember that, in the Netherlands, retired workers are guaranteed income of 80% of their work pay.

There has also been a disturbing pattern in some unions of officers who use the benefits fund as a kind of personal slush fund, taking luxury trips to "educational" conferences, for example, or collecting extra salaries as a trustee of the fund or using the funds as a source of patronage, hiring relatives as employees or contractors. The gruesome spectacle at the end of 2019 of a parade of United Auto Workers officers headed for court or to jail for misusing the funds is a stain on our movement. Every member in locals with these funds is affected so their administration is a constant topic of discussion. Administer the funds properly and honestly, and avoid doing anything that might cause an eyebrow to be raised.Always make sure the members get prompt and pleasant service from the benefits office.

Having excellent benefit funds is a HUGE organizing incentive for non-union workers in many industries, who have no health care, disability or retirement benefits.

*10) Physical plant.*If your union owns a hall, you need to pay particular attention to the expenses involved, especially if you own an old building with a leaking roof or ancient heating system. Look at the expense of this building the way you look at the expenses of your house, divided between routine maintenance and capital improvements. Does the hall meet the needs of your membership today? Many unions have lost significant membership but still maintain enormous buildings. Other unions are still paying rent, even though the local is stable and could look at buying its own facility. In other cases, locals have bought buildings and have become landlords, providing income (along with the headaches of dealing with tenants).

With the shifting of work locations, is your union hall close to the members' work site? It needs to be convenient for your members. If your workplace has moved, you should consider moving the union offices as well.

In all cases, reach out to your membership and make them understand that the building belongs to them—not to "the union"—and explain how the finances work and strive to make the hall a center of all kinds of activities. One new officer found that making the union hall and office into a non-smoking area created controversy. Clearly smoke, even second-hand smoke, is both unpleasant and dangerous, but some die-hard smoking members may claim that their constitutional rights have been infringed if butts are banned. Do it anyway.

As part of your local's strategic planning, look at your space needs and the most efficient way to build membership involvement. If you are considering the purchase or construction of a building, location is very important: a union hall that is far away or has lousy parking or other problems will not encourage the members to come on in.

Does your union hall or offices need a technological upgrade? Does your staff have good computers and full internet? One new officer said that "cleaning out 20 years of old computers and monitors" was important, as well as safely disposing of even older equipment that had been simply stashed in a closet at the union hall.

Can you show videos or PowerPoints to your members at a meeting? Is there a decent sound system so the officers and members can speak to each other without screaming?

Look also at the regular maintenance of your buildings. Some new officers found that custodial contracts were given to family members or friends of the ousted officers, often at exorbitant rates.

11) Union staff—servicing and clerical. This is a HUGE challenge for every new officer because both groups of union workers, servicing and clerical, can help the union run well, or can sink it. You also probably found that servicing assignments were a campaign issue—certain members thought the rep was lazy or incompetent but was protected by the officers, based on personal loyalties rather than on skills and abilities. Now the union is a boss, so do the right thing by your workers, but also make certain that the staff understands the changes in the local and that they are ready and capable of serving the membership. You need to develop job goals and descriptions so everyone is clear about what is supposed to happen and establish pay and benefit scales that are logical, and not based upon favoritism and self-enrichment.

Servicing staff—for most of your members, the fulltime servicing reps, business agents, or whatever the title in your union, are the face of the union, so you need to make sure that they have the skills and motivation to do their jobs, and that they understand the new thinking involved in The Organizing Model. Staff assignments fit the skills of the staff and the needs of the membership because sometimes the old officers made assignments based on political loyalty. The most difficult challenge is getting rid of staff who cannot make the change. One new local officer described keeping "an Old Joe rep in the background until he could be persuaded to retire."

In another situation, a local had to grapple with whether to retain a rep who had lost his driver's license because of a DUI but expected to continue on regular assignments. A local should be a model employer and, in a case like this, could offer counselling, or an EAP program while making an effort to accommodate the rep's inability to drive. Obviously, the stress of a union job has pushed many people into alcoholism, or into other health or emotional situations, so a new officer may need to deal with this challenge.

In drastic situations, you may need to terminate a rep who can't, or won't, do the job. This situation can get very messy because the rep may have friends and supporters and may even be protected by his or her own union contract so all of the strategic skills of a new officer will be quickly tested. At the same time, you were elected to make changes so, as Davy Crockett always said, "Be sure you're right and then go ahead."

Look at the servicing assignments to see what changes need to be made. If you have an amalgamated local, some officers may prefer certain staff members and you should try to accommodate them unless the preference is based on personal loyalties rather than union strength. Are there contentious relations between a staff rep and certain bosses, maybe based on old grudges? If so, a fresh face may be helpful to your members.

It is a good investment to send your staff for training in basic union skills and also in the use of technology. As we saw in Chapter 3, everyone needs to change—the election results showed how the membership feels and all of the union's employees, as well as the new officers, need to hear the message.

Clerical staff—just as important as the servicing reps, the clerical staff needs to have both the motivation and the skills to support the changes in the union. Once again, many new officers find that the office staff was hired for family relations or political obligations and may not be willing or able to take on new responsibilities. Looking at the work practices in the office, so the flow of material is logically organized, is a critical task. Other new officers have found that the institutional knowledge of longtime clerical (and servicing) staff is enormous and all in their heads. Capturing this knowledge and making it available to everyone is very important. At the same time, cross-training your clerical staff is important. A new officer found that only one person, now 76 years old, knew how to track incoming dues and pay the various *per capitas*. Bringing other staff into the process is necessary.

12) *Union vendors or consultants.* Most large unions have outside contractors to provide specialized services, everything from legal advice to printing to coffee supplies. As a new officer, you need to know who these outside contractors are, how they got retained and how effective they are. It is especially important if you rely on lawyers because their advice, and their fee structures, can be both important and controversial. In many locals, a law firm recognizes that an officer can cut them off a juicy retainer, or a lucrative per-hour fee schedule, and so the lawyers feel that their function is to provide legal justification, or cover, for an officer. In too many cases, bad decisions are presented to the members with a letter from the lawyer, endorsing the bad decision or proclaiming it to be legal. You need to look at the history—how much was a law firm paid, what did they do and are they worth the money? It is also very important as a new officer to not let the lawyers run your local, as many officers are willing to do. You were elected to make decisions—so step up.

For other union vendors, look at the contracts to see if you are getting good bang for your buck. One new officer found that the local's insurance carrier—from auto coverage to workers' compensation—was being sued for embezzlement and was related, by marriage, to the current business manager. Even beyond an obviously crooked situation, consider opening up for bid some of the outside services to see what's available. In the end, you may keep the same vendor but at least you will be certain that you are getting the best value for your members.

There is also a very different kind of challenge for some new officers—those who have just organized for the first time and either have a new local, or a new unit in an existing amalgamated local. For workers like you, Old Joe never lived so you have to learn everything about unionism for the first time, and it can be almost overwhelming, especially if you are negotiating your first contract. The bad news is that you have to develop a whole new set of skills, but the good news is that you have not been surrounded by officers with bad habits. Reading this book will give you a start but try to read as much as you can, talk with as many experienced union officers as possible, ask questions of your staff rep who's doing your negotiations—you have a lot of challenges ahead but it beats being non-union.

13) *Union Education and Training Programs*—Last but certainly not least, as a new officer you should plan that every member goes to a union education activity at least twice a year. It is a huge challenge since most unions have dismal, or non-existent, education programs, a reflection of The Servicing Model.

Many officers regard this kind of education program as a threat—not a threat to the union but a threat to their continued occupation of a union office. A president of a Central Labor Council once asked: "Why should I send any member to a training class? Then they'll just run against me for office."

You could train your members in all of the topics in this chapter, emphasizing the importance of their participation in the union. Basic classes in your union contract, in the benefit funds, and in the history of your union are great openings for your members, and will attract new enthusiasm and new participants.

In the next chapter, we will look at Communications but setting up an on-line union education program, with courses and webinars, is one way to use new technology to reach members who may be spread out—even nationwide—or work various shifts so that getting all of them in one room at one time for an extended class is impossible.

Now Go Do It!

TASKS:

1) Make a list of all of the tasks that your union handles, using circles to help diagram all of the activities. If you are affected by a district or international union, list its functions as well, letting the circles overlap if there is shared responsibility. For example, use a big circle for Grievances, and calculate which areas are handled by the local, by the District or by the International.

2) Evaluate each task in terms of who does and who pays.

3) Judge each task in terms of current membership involvement.

4) Figure out the potential for membership involvement of each task, and what changes you need to make to increase your membership's participation.

5) Evaluate all employees of the union to see what training they might require or whether they should continue in their present positions.

6) Use your strategic planning skills to create Action Plans for each of the tasks.

6 THE FINANCES OF THE UNION
"Money talks—loud! Not having money talks louder." —The Great Authority

There is no question that one of the most difficult and most dangerous areas for a new union officer involves the money of the union—where it comes from, where it goes and, most important, who decides how it is spent. It is an area for the new officer to study carefully because this is one area where all of the issues around making decisions come to an often abrupt climax. If many marriages fail due to arguments over money, the same can be true for a local union.

If new information is essential for the new officer, the financial information is *most* essential. While the union's accounting system may appear to be complex and convoluted, the new officer can approach the books as if they were individual checking accounts—income and expenses. Dealing realistically with your money (after all, the union's treasury belongs to the *members* and not to the officers) is an important step in becoming a good union officer.

Directing money for your priorities may be a wrenching experience, a drastic and dramatic change, but most unions are confronting financial problems. Just as most workers are facing financial decisions in their personal lives, the sooner you get the union's money under control, the better.

Unfortunately, in The Servicing Model of Unionism, union finances are often a mystery to the members, who fail to acquire a fundamental sense of the union's operations. It is very curious and, at the same time, quite common for workers who worry about every penny of their household budgets to know nothing about the way their union spends their money. On the other hand, one source of dissatisfaction among some members about paying dues has been that no one gets a thorough accounting of where their money goes.

The understanding of the union's finances, then, is tied to the union's strategy for success and survival. All ideas are good ideas until you have to pay for them, so let's look at the financial structure of an average union to see how it functions.

A union's income is derived from several sources, but mainly from the membership dues. If the union has contracts with *union security agreements*, these contracts require that any worker covered by the contract must pay either full dues or a servicing fee to the union.

The dues structure varies widely from union to union: some unions have a strict dues structure of so many

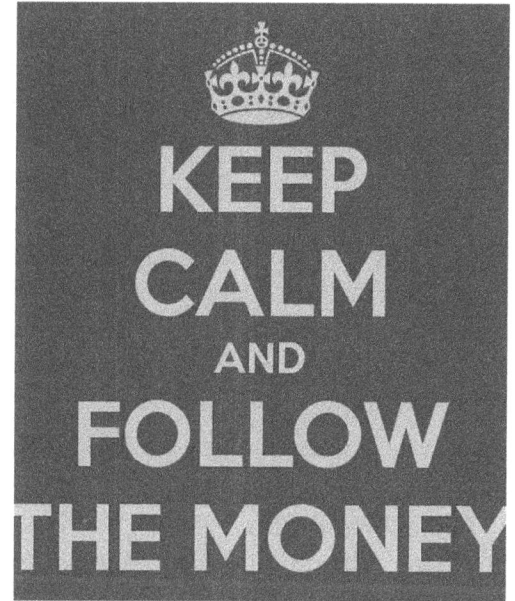

dollars per week or month. These locals must then go to the membership for every dues increase, often a bruising political battle.

Other unions have instituted *a percent formula*, making dues a percentage of the worker's wages; in some cases, dues are calculated only on straight-time earnings while other unions collect dues on overtime as well. In other unions, dues are calculated as a certain number of hours per month so that as wages go up, so does the union's dues income.

Another controversial source of union income is the initiation fee charged of new members, so you probably paid it when you first got hired. Many officers have seen their treasuries grow substantially from these fees, especially in industries like retail where a lot of temporary workers come on for the summer, pay the full initiation fee and then leave. Some of the building trades have very high initiation fees, limiting potential applicants. On the other hand, every organizer can tell you that waiving the initiation fee for new locals is an important part of any campaign, because the Boss tries to portray The Union as a money grubber and fat cat.

In most cases, the dues are collected by a *check-off* method: a worker signs a written authorization to the boss who deducts the dues on a regular basis and is then supposed to remit to the union the dues collected. As a point of information, and one which is often confused by union officers, no contract requires that a worker use the check-off procedures; the contract language simply requires that the worker be a "member in good standing," so the worker may elect to pay dues through the check-off provision, but also may elect to pay directly to the union.

It is obviously more convenient for the union to have its members on the check-off, but unions for years hand collected dues through the steward system. In many ways, the hand collection increased the organizing of a union local because union officers had to meet regularly with every member, and the members developed leverage in controlling their officers. While hand collection of dues appears to be difficult and cumbersome, it can be done.

Many unions have recently proven this point as they struggle to resolve negotiations by working without a contract. If a union has tough negotiations, cannot reach a new agreement and is unwilling to strike, the local members continue to work while negotiations continue. The boss will try to get some leverage by canceling the contract, starting with the check-off to try to strangle the union financially and create dissension, although recent court and National Labor Relations Board decisions have ruled that the requirement that an employer maintain conditions also includes the check-off. The skill of working without a contract is a whole different topic, as described in Jerry Tucker's book, *The Inside Game*: what you need to know is that the cancellation of the check-off may be simply one obstacle to be overcome.

For most unions, the *dues remittance* is sent directly to the local union, which then sends on *per capita*

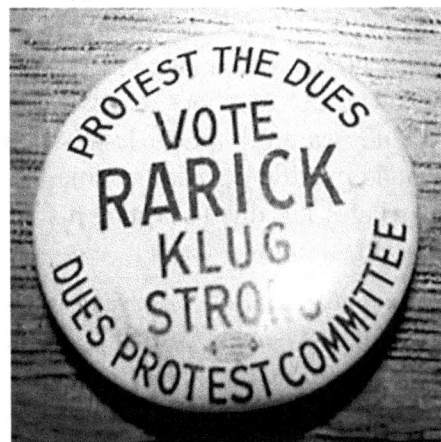

(Latin for "each head," literally), often called *per caps*, to the international and district or other union bodies. The financial advantage to the local is that it has the money sooner. One political advantage is the threat to hold back per capita if the higher union levels are not doing what they are supposed to do—not providing servicing assistance, or cutting back on organizing.

In other unions, such as the Steelworkers, however, the dues are sent directly to the International Union, which keeps its share and sends the local its share. Some international unions are chronically slow in making these payments, provoking difficulties for the local in meeting its own financial obligations.

One hazard for the union, at all levels, is a delay in retrieving the funds from the check-off. A boss with financial problems, or a boss who is trying to gain an edge over the union, will delay remitting the check-off to the union so it is essential to have someone from the union assigned to track these dues obligations, especially in an amalgamated local with many employers. Jump on any late payments so that the amount does not accumulate. The local can begin both legal and organizational proceedings to force the boss to do what he has agreed to do in the contract. Any delay can create problems for a union that is dependent on a steady revenue source, the equivalent of living paycheck to paycheck for an individual worker. If your union lives, in effect, paycheck to paycheck, however, it is time to look at a complete overhaul of your operations.

Dues income in open shop states can become a major variable, because workers covered by the contract are not required to be union members (=pay dues) but get all the benefits of the union contract and can demand union representation. Members who are unhappy, for example, with a new contract can parade their dissatisfaction by dropping out. A succession of anti-union politicians, like Scott Walker in Wisconsin or Bruce Rauner in Illinois who ran for office promising to break unions, and a parade of court cases, like *Janus v AFSCME*, have also devastated this steady income.

So, you, as a new officer, have to look both at the financial aspect of the non-members, and figure how changes could affect your union budget, as well as planning internal organizing campaigns to sign them up to both build leverage and to improve the local's financial numbers. In Chapter 9, you will get a discussion of the Duty of Fair Representation because protecting non-members is very controversial.

So that's money coming into your union. How about the money going out?

Once you have figured out how, and how much, income arrives at your local, evaluate how money is spent. Some of your expenses are fixed: your *per capita* payments are one obvious expense. Other fixed expenses, as in your household, are obvious. If you own a building or pay rent you have these fixed payments, such as utilities and salaries for any full-time staff and clerical workers.

New officers who come directly out of the membership without having spent some time on the Executive Board of the union likely have no idea of the union's financial situation. Even then, in many unions the top officers treat the union's finances, and especially their expenses, as a point of royal privilege—don't ask, don't tell! One crisis for new officers is looking at the financial arrangements of previous officers because you may find significant financial irregularities—personal expenses charged off to the union, expense checks paid without proper documentation.

One local union officer remarked, "We had to learn to keep up with the W-4's, the payroll, the taxes, the 401-k's, the audits, the standing bills, the multiple investment accounts and the various insurance and fiduciary policies. It was a lot to pick up."

You should not be intimidated, especially because so much of the union finances are publicly available on-line. As a result of The Labor-Management Reporting and Disclosure Act of 1959 (LMRDA), all private sector unions are required to file an annual LM-2 report, and they are all posted on the Department of Labor's web site (www.dol.gov).Ironically, this requirement often discourages public sector unions from trying to organize private contractors. In fact, an anti-union campaign called The Center for Union Facts, headed by Richard Berman has been promoting its access to union financial reports as part of its attack. According to Citizens for Responsibility and Ethics in Washington, (https://www.citizens-forethics.org/) "The Center harasses, attacks, and undermines labor unions. CUF works hand in hand with business interests that oppose unionization of their employees and receives support from an array of foundations in order to diminish the economic and political power of unions. CUF founder Richard Berman views himself as a participant in a 'long-term war' against unions, dating to his early career as a union-busting lawyer. CUF performs opposition research against unions and runs hyperbolic ad campaigns that have compared union leaders to dictators and tyrants."

So get a grip on the union's finances, even if it means going back to the members who helped you get elected to win support for opening the books. The greater the resistance of the old officers, the more likely it is that the financial examination will overturn some pretty big rocks with some pretty big worms underneath. Your position is simple: you want to know what the officers do with the members' money. Ask the local financial officer to walk you through the books, explaining to you everything you need to know. If the officer shifts you off to the union's accountant, then make an appointment with the accountant to go through the books.

One warning: just because someone is an accountant, it doesn't mean that the person will give you the truth. Court cases involving accounting firms are glowing proof of this because evidence reveals that some accountants simply support the shady bookkeeping of officers, rather than providing an independent evaluation. The accountant, who is hired by the union officers and wants to keep this job, may be inclined to cover up certain bad practices. In recent years, the careless or crooked accountant has become more exposed, so don't assume anything about your accountant. Demand to see the figures and make your own judgments.

Remember that the accountant is simply responsible for the figures. All decisions to do with money are the responsibility of the local through procedures provided by the local bylaws. The accounting for the union's finances is tightly controlled by federal requirements, so keeping track of income and expenses is not just good union practice, it's the law—and the penalties for violating the law can be severe.

Dealing with the union finances is very important to the local's strategic planning. It is a symptom of poor leadership to avoid any discussion of financial changes until a crisis hits the union. If a boss is talking about layoffs, or if there are significant drops in employment, the union officers should move pro-actively to adjust the union's expenses, rather than draining any savings accounts. The failure to adjust to reduced income can become a crisis for many unions. It's a mistake for officers to continue to spend on salaries and expenses as if employment and income were steady.

Legislation in Wisconsin in 2015, in West Virginia in 2016 and Kentucky in 2017, brought the open shop to those states, while court decisions like *Janus v AFSCME*, in 2018, which blocked "fair share" agreements in the public sector, brought a significant drop in union membership. Reversing this lousy legislation is obviously a priority but, until it happens, you need to take a hard look at your finances. Spend the members' dues money wisely on activities that will strengthen the union and which will be attractive to the new, and reluctant, dues-payers.

Another example of sudden financial challenges for union officers came in November, 2019, when the Department of Veterans Administration decreed that Union representatives at the VA will have severe restrictions on their ability to perform union work. The VA announced that unions will have to pay for office space and equipment use and representatives will have to spend 75 percent of their time doing non-union work. Most notably, the rule change notes that the agency will not approve "taxpayer-funded union time for preparing or pursuing grievances, including arbitration, on behalf of bargaining unit employees," according to the *Federal Times*. In a press release, the VA claimed in fiscal year 2016 the department spent more than $49 million on employee compensation for union reps to work more than a "million duty hours on taxpayer-funded union time." Even if this figure is an exaggeration—what? The Trump Administration distort facts?—the new policy represents a major financial challenge to federal unions.

Unionism for the past 60 years or so has been dependent on a steady stream of dues income, allowing the unions to function with some financial stability. Those days are gone, but many union officers are unwilling to face reality. There has been a culture of money that has been very destructive to the spirit of unionism. Members, for example, expect to be paid *lost time* for every union activity, from organizing to political action to social functions. Some members even get the unsavory nickname of "lost time artist," so you need to cut back on unnecessary payments to these members. This expectation of being fully compensated for every union activity is one of the main characteristics of The Servicing Model of Unionism that you are committed to change.

Any study of workers' history brings up one important contrast: in the past, workers participated in their unions, which were social movements reaching out to the community around the workplace where most of the workers lived. Since the early unions had no financial resources, if a union was going to function and grow, the members had to volunteer. Don't forget that workers were working longer hours for much less money in these early days, so they had to build their unions out of an emotional commitment—the kind of dedication that money can't buy. So don't let your members slide away with their excuses of "I'm just too busy."

As unions became more established, and financial resources began to grow, this sense of participation diminished. The members became dependent on full-time paid officers and staff—who themselves encouraged this trend—and these full-timers' value to the union seemed to grow. The question of the union's finances, then, is absolutely tied to the functioning of the union itself and is the best reason for the new officer to get a firm grip on the union's finances—past, present, and future.

The new officer should also examine the union's financial past—how things were last year, five years ago, ten years ago—and should look at the future, to evaluate where the union expects to be financially in a year or two or ten. This financial planning is an essential part of your Strategic Plan, since an idea is good only if there is money to pay for it.

There may be some tough decisions to make but often your members will pull together to keep the union strong. In one training I did for the ATU, a small local with a small bank account was faced with the challenge of paying for an important arbitration case. The membership voted unanimously for a 6-month assessment to cover the expense, an inspiring effort.

One argument often made by union officers who want to spend every cent of income is that the union is not a company and therefore should not have to show a profit. Often this line is an excuse to spend excessively and recklessly, for example, on individual expenses or outings for a select group, rather than facing today's financial realities. A union should operate the way a household operates. Setting aside money for savings is an excellent idea as long as the basic functions (and this phrase is widely open to interpretation!) are not neglected.

What's left to argue about?

There is a lot to argue about, especially if there are full-time union staff or officers, or considerable expenses for "travel and entertainment." You need to figure out who is paid, what they are paid, what expenses have been approved, and by whom. Travel and meals are reimbursable for union business but are often abused. In these times, it is proper to ask whether a particular trip was really necessary, or whether some expenses are justified.

One area of controversy is the hosting of union conferences or conventions. The practice has been to send a few members to a fancy hotel or resort, paying not only lost time and travel, but also providing amenities— hospitality rooms, banquets, excursions--that seen outrageous in these tough times.

In many cases, local union bylaws provide guidelines and even spending limits—the spending of a local officer is limited to a certain amount without the approval of the Executive Board and/or the full membership. Check to see if such guidelines exist and whether they have been obeyed. If you find abuses, you will be confronted with screams of outrage if you begin to question unjustified expenses, so hang tough. The union at all levels must operate in a financially sound manner in order to support its programs, and members with fixed dues are very reluctant to vote for an increase. Get a good sense of the union's finances; establish your political priorities and then figure out if the union treasury will stretch to support these priorities.

One group of new officers found that contracts for luxurious staff cars were a huge financial burden for the local so they cut them off and used modest cars, both saving money and presenting a better look to the members.

One major change could be the elimination of union credit cards, which are easily misused. If officers, or members, have an expense, let them pay for it on their own credit cards and submit the receipts for reimbursement; this allows you to avoid even the appearance of impropriety. One local in Baltimore, for example, was thrown into bitter conflict because an officer at a convention charged $3,000.00 of personal expenses on his union credit card, claiming he had misplaced his personal card. Yes, he insisted that he had intended to repay all of the charges but the appearance of impropriety was a catastrophe.

One of the sorriest spectacles in our movement was the procession of UAW officers—including the current and former presidents of the international union—into court on charges of stealing enormous amounts of money, or of using dues money for extravagant personal expenses. Even worse is the sense that other UAW officers must have known about these thefts and said nothing. Still worse is that this corruption may have affected the union's position in national negotiations with major auto manufacturers that brought severe concessions to UAW members. Indeed, money talks! Anti-union advocates pounce on every incident to try to damage the whole movement.

Let's look at union finances as an organizing tool. How can you bring the membership into the discussion of money?

The best way is to keep saying, "The union's money belongs to the members." The money for "The Union" did not appear out of thin air—your members created all funds by paying dues and initiation fees, and often approved the creation of special funds, like a building fund or social fund, through voluntary assessments.

Many officers seem to have forgotten this point, and deal with the members in the same way they deal with the boss: as adversaries. Every member complains at one time or another about paying dues, so take this negative and turn it around as a method for increasing membership involvement.

One good way is to publish a regular financial report for the members. One local for which I worked, as a tradition, issued a written quarterly report, itemizing every check paid by the local with an indication of what the money went for. The first objection to such a procedure, of course, is that the boss will get a copy of it and will know what the union does with its money.

So what?

In the first place, the boss simply has to go to the same Department of Labor site on the internet to get your LM-2. Changes by the Department of Labor in 2005 imposed even stricter requirements on union financial accounting as a kind of punishment for labor's political activities. Using this form, your employer will have a pretty good sense of what's going on. More important, if your local finances are in good shape, and you are packing away money into a strike fund, for example, then the boss can see that you are armed and ready for the next contract negotiations.

It is critical that new officers understand forms like the LM-2 because accounting for the union's money—to the members and to the government—is important. Still more important, making the union's finances an area for discussion will only *increase* membership involvement. It proves that the elected officers have nothing to hide and that the union's priorities are being discussed and funded, so one source of discontent and dissension is eliminated.

You can argue all you want about the unfairness of this attention on the union expenditures while your boss is able to hide many of his expenditures, even from the stockholders in a public company or from the taxpayers in the case of a public agency. Thanks to federal law, it's a reality. More importantly, it is just good union practice to be smart and honest about the members' money. You'll have to deal with it.

Finally, another area of concern is union investments, especially after the Great Recession of 2007-09. If your union is lucky enough to have money in the bank, or administers a pension or benefit fund, you always try to make money but, as interest rates declined, more and more unions—and their financial advisers—desperately tried to maintain income by getting into some very risky financial gambles. As a result, many funds lost money—after all, Wall Street is the biggest casino going, and at a gambling table, no one wins unless someone loses.

Now Go Do It!

TASKS:

1) Get a thorough look at your union's financial position, including income and expenses.

2) How does this compare with last year? Five years ago?

3) What does the future look like? Do you have any major expenditures planned?

4) Based on its spending, what have been your local union's financial priorities?

5) How do you report the union's finances to your members?

6) What changes should and could be made?

7 BUILDING A COMMUNICATIONS NETWORK
"The single biggest problem in communication is the illusion that it has taken place." — George Bernard Shaw

One important area of membership participation is an organized system of communications among the members and officers. If you were elected as an outsider candidate, you have already learned some of the most important methods of getting out *The Word* to your co-workers because you created a new network to spread the word about your own candidacy. Now you have to try to expand your one-time campaign communications into a regular system to both give and get information and opinions.

Remember that communications—*real* union communications— require a two-way conversation, involving both speaking (or writing or posting) and listening—really listening, not just going through the motions of sticking out your ears and nodding your head.

In a perfect world, the officers of the local would expect to improve communications with the members. Alas, the world is not perfect, as the chart on The Servicing Model of Unionism [*Appendix 1*] demonstrates. Many officers only want one-way communications: from themselves on high down to the lowly members, like marching orders. No wonder the members felt left out of their local and voted for you! As a new officer, you must change this pattern, either by getting the local as a whole to expand its communications network or by going it alone and setting up your own communications system.

Readers of this book consistently indicate that improving communications is their greatest challenge, especially as electronic communications have grown. After all, how many of your co-workers—especially the younger ones—don't have phones and know how to text, to tweet, to post photos instantly? Even the geezers have figured out e-mail and Facebook, so make social media work to build your local.

The challenge, of course, is that there is no control over these communications—any member can post any opinion or piece of Fake News. Since it is fast and easy for members to communicate with each other, you might as well encourage these dialogues within the union structure, so that the officers will at least be able to see—and possibly challenge—malicious rumors or anti-union comments.

If your union has members in more than one location, the challenge of establishing quick and accurate communications is even more important because the spreading out of the union is an invitation for the starting of all sorts of rumors—the archenemy of solidarity.

Generally, in a local there are several formal ways for the officers and members to communicate with each other. By "formal" I mean a method of communication which seems to have both structure and regularity, in

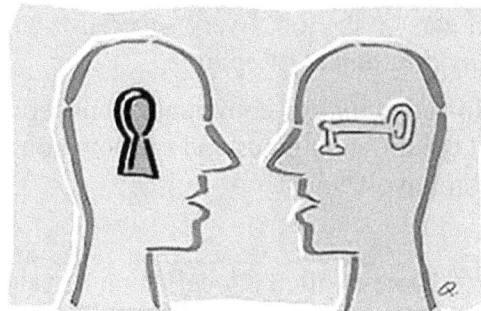

contrast to the millions of informal ways that workers spread *The Word*—on the job, during breaks and social occasions, in car pools and outside the workplace through the explosive avenues of social media.

In many locals, the newsletter or leaflet distribution generally expresses the officers' position. It is very common to refer to these messages as "The Union," as if pronouncements by the officers represent the sentiments of each and every member.

Despite their feelings to the contrary, elected union officers are not "The Union."Unions do not speak as one voice—there are questions and disagreements, just as there are within a family. While some of these disagreements may be troublesome, or even destructive to the union, they can be a healthy part of a membership organization. One objection raised by many officers to allowing differing opinions in official union publications is the claim that the boss will know we are divided, as if the boss doesn't have a thousand sets of ears on the job. Every supervisor and snitch is reporting back on a regular basis, so it's pretty hard to hide any differences of opinion.

So-called *official* communications represent different ways in which pronouncements are issued so let's look at the different types and see how you, as a new officer, can make effective use of them to increase membership involvement.

- There is often a local union newsletter, magazine or leaflet, regularly distributed to the members. While printed materials may seem so primitive, they do have real value, increasing visibility and getting out important ideas at key times. Remember that the act of passing out these leaflets is a way to build membership involvement: if you have 200 leaflets to pass out and you distribute all of them yourself, then you have not increased membership involvement at all. Get your members involved with the process. In one local, for example, an officer referred to stewards, and to another group, as "leaflet-hander-outers."

- There are so-called union bulletin boards placed throughout your workplace; we call them "so-called" union bulletin boards because, as defined in your union contract, there can be some pretty severe restrictions on who can post notices and what these notices can say. In some cases, the bulletin boards are inside glass cases, and only the boss has a key, which the local union officers must request.

- There are the local union meetings, which are supposed to involve reports and discussions.

- As the expense and difficulties of producing a newsletter increase, more locals are moving into electronic communications and host local websites, which often replace the printed communications. When your local opens its web site, be sure to include a message board so that your members can post their feelings for all to see. Be prepared for a negative reaction from some of the old officers, whose careers have been based upon ignoring the wishes of their members.

Some unions, and candidates for union office, have included videos in these communications—it's easy and it's free, so why not? A terrific feature of a web site are short videos from longtime members, describing the

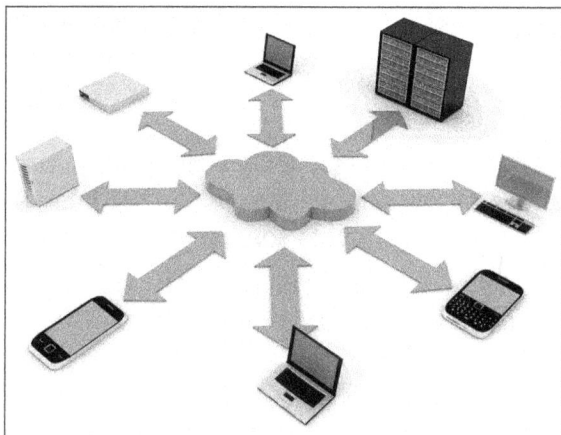

importance of the union and especially targeting new members who have no union experience. These new members may think that the benefits they get under the contract have dropped from the sky, so they need to hear the history of how the old timers fought to achieve them.

Many incumbent officers will oppose any efforts to increase participation in running the union. As a member, you may have tried to create a program to increase membership involvement but you felt as if you were shouting in an empty forest because no one seemed to hear you. Maybe you tried to get a statement, or some sort of report included in your local union's official publication, but the editor told you either that there is no room or insisted on editing your article so that it reversed what you want to say. So, this door was closed. If you are functioning under The Servicing Model of Unionism, you probably won't get access to the so-called "union" bulletin boards either because management will help your officers muffle your statements.

No matter what happens, and no matter how frustrated you get by the obstacles thrown into your path, always look for ways to communicate directly with your members who elected you. This means both finding new ways of communication and overcoming the possible opposition of other officers who may see this activity as a threat, not as a way to rebuild the local. After all, members who begin to participate in their union's activities are all potential candidates to run for office, right?

You can stand up at a membership meeting and demand to be heard, but often your opponents will use parliamentary procedures or just plain intimidation to keep you from speaking.

Are you stuck? If you can't have access to these formal communications sources, do you simply have to keep still? You do if you simply follow established methods of communications. But you got elected by not following established methods of communications, right? By doing things differently? And didn't your membership respond? As a new officer, it is essential—if you have not done so already—to tap into the informal networks, which can be very powerful, as any union organizer of new workplaces can confirm.

The most important element of your election campaign was your organizing committee—the groups of friends and supporters who helped you get your issues out and maybe even helped pay for some of the expenses through voluntary donations. No matter what these active people did in the campaign, they began to change the culture of the local by expanding membership participation. They helped you decentralize your union, bringing up issues in every informal meeting place—in the bathrooms, on the job, in the parking lot or wash-up rooms.

Keep this activity going.

Meet with these supporters and tell them that the campaign has not really finished even though the votes have been counted. Develop a positive direction for your union and a more aggressive attitude toward problems at work. After all, your campaign was about changing your union, not just about getting you elected.

When you ran for office, you used all kinds of tactics to communicate with your members—leaflets, small meetings, maybe even a website or e-mail list, or other electronic communications. Now that you are in office, these alternate and unofficial methods of communications are classic elements of The Organizing Model of Unionism. As part of their self-improvement efforts, many union officers have started attending workshops run by groups like LabourStart or by labor studies programs, for example, to learn these new techniques. In many cases your employer may even be a part of a global corporation, so your communications needs are international. Learn how to SKYPE or FaceTime and use social networking to help you build solidarity and leverage.

Create a regular newsletter of your own—a kind of officer's report. Allow room for others to offer their opinions, like a Letters to the Editor column. Make your newsletter a method for reaching out to every worker on every important issue.

One very effective zoneman in a Baltimore Steelworkers local created a zone newsletter listing all of the grievances on a regular schedule, any current negotiations or problems, and some opinions. He created this newsletter on his own, had it printed and passed it out. He was compensating for the lack of interest by the local officers in letting the members in on the usual grievance activities. Not only did the members in this zone feel more involved in the union, the representative never found a problem in getting re-elected! Some good deeds do get rewarded.

As a sign of the times, his successor in the same mill recreated the zone report and distributed it electronically, as well as in print. He solicited the home e-mail addresses of the members to get the material out effectively and had 700 cell phone numbers stored for text messages. Other officers have created websites—so simple our kids can show us how—that are a great way to list grievance activity.

One important aspect about building an electronic communications network is to use only the private e-mail addresses of your members. Too often, officers want to take the easy way out and send notices to the work e-mail addresses of their members, especially at public-sector workplaces where work e-mails are easy to collect. This is a dangerous practice: not only can an employer block any messages, shutting down your network, but the employer also has the right to read any of the communications and to discipline workers who use work time and equipment to read personal messages about their union. With so many smart phones and other devices in use today, get your members' information and bypass the boss altogether. Sure, there will be members who insist that they don't want to be "bothered" by union messages but you will get the majority of your members, especially at contract negotiations time. One large union in Minnesota has even begun to use this electronic system to collect union dues, bypassing again the employer and the usual procedure. Remember, there is no more normal.

Continue small group meetings on a regular basis, such as a lunch-and-learn, to create an organization among your members. While meetings may be just fine for passing information from you to the members, remember that your main task is to build an organization at work and to create a kind of new union within the structure of the old.

Needless to say, you have to have some sort of a program that goes beyond simply bringing more members into participation. If you have a disagreement with the incumbent officers about your right as a new officer to participate in local decisions, you have to be careful that your disputes do not appear to be simple personality issues or post-election bitterness. In such a case, your disputes sink to the level of a personal pissing match, a spectacle that reflects the worst elements of unionism and which will certainly discourage membership participation.

There is one other important method of communication which you apparently have discovered or you would not have run such a successful campaign. This technique is called *one-on-one*, and it is simply one member talking in detail with another member. The one-on-one is the foundation for all good organizing in any organization, and the time spent turning one influential workplace leader in your direction is worth the time spent passing out leaflets to one thousand.

And remember what you learned in the chapter on strategic planning. Make communications a priority, plan how to do it, be proactive, and evaluate your plan as you go along. And remember that the most important word in communications is spelled L-I-S-T-E-N. Do not focus so much on getting your opinions out that you neglect everyone else's.

While it may be a broad application of the word "communication," increasing union visibility is also important. Wear your union insignia—button, shirt, cap—at work and at home so people know you're Union Proud. Walk by a union construction site and you will see union decals on hard hats. Get union bumper stickers and encourage every member to put one on a car. Some unions have negotiated to wear union patches on their uniforms—and even got the company to pay for them. Get all of your members to show as well. One IBEW local in Chicago even created a Proud Union Home yard sign.

Now Go Do It!

TASKS:

1) Evaluate the existing communications now in place for both your union and your employer. How many people read them, if they are written, or listen, or even watch them, if you have video communications?

2) Which of these methods of communications are open to you, as a new officer?

3) Which ones are open to individual members? How do your individual members get their opinions heard?

4) What methods of communications were helpful to you in your election campaign? Have you tried to continue them or have you let them lapse?

5) Have you ever tried a formal one-on-one campaign?

6) Do you still have a decentralized network that will help you get out the word to yourco-workers?

7) How many members are "wired"—that is, have computers or e-mail, making an electronic communications network possible?

8 UNDERSTANDING THE LEGAL FRAMEWORK
NLRB. OSHA. FMLA. ADA. DOL. FMCS. ERISA. LM-2. ALJ. DFR. PBGC. WARN. UC. NFL. R2D2.

Do these acronyms and abbreviations mean anything to you? Mostly not, I suspect.

Unions in the United States are some of the country's most closely regulated institutions, covered by literally thousands of pages of laws, regulations, executive orders, judicial decisions and just plain political BS. You simply need to know that, in the United States, government at all levels has basically been co-opted by the bosses to strictly control the determination of people like us to build labor organizations. The history of these restrictions, and a strategy to get rid of them, is a topic certainly worth pursuing but, as a new officer, you must first play the hand you have been dealt.

This chapter is in no way a substitute for an extensive course in labor and employment law, combined with experience dealing with the law at different levels. In fact, a project for any new officer is to have at least a one-day workshop on the laws that apply to local unions so that you will be aware of what they are and whom you should call with a question. You should get a very brief view of some of the important laws to alert you to their existence and to warn you to step carefully.

If it is not practical for you to immediately take some course in labor law, then go to *Appendix 5* of this book where you will at least get an introduction to the various federal laws and reporting requirements that you need to follow. If you represent only public sector workers, then many of the laws, such as the National Labor Relations Act, do not apply to you because they cover only specific private sector workers. If your union has been a public sector union and has begun to organize private sector workers—as many ATU locals are doing, for example—then the NLRA will apply to you and you better study up on it.

Crossing the law can lead you to political embarrassment, to lawsuits from your boss, the government, or from unhappy members (or non-members), to considerable expense and, most important, to a diversion of your meager time and resources into battles you don't need to fight at this time. As you learn about the hazards of some of the laws, you will get a great introduction to political action—if a law is harmful to you and your members, make it a political campaign. Our chances for legal success are dramatically dropping as more conservative judges are appointed. In September, 2019, Senator Lindsey Graham bragged that 150 new appointees had been confirmed in less than 3 years of the Trump administration, about half as many as Obama appointed in 8 years. "As Chairman of the Senate Judiciary Committee, I will continue to push through highly qualified, conservative judges at all levels of the federal courts," he said in a statement. "These conservative judicial appointments will impact our nation for years to come."

As a new officer in a union that represents public workers, you need to find out what laws your state or local jurisdiction has passed to control unions. Or to eliminate them—the state of Virginia, for example, in 1993 joined North Carolina as the only two states to totally prohibit public sector collective bargaining (and both are open shop states—no surprise).

There are also many "employment" laws—like workers compensation, disability discrimination, WARN—which may affect your members so you need to both learn about them and keep up to date on any changes.

Getting confused? Other officers have figured it out, so you can—and will.

Remembering all the functions of the union, there are basically three types of laws that cover our activities:
• The union as a representative of its members, with laws that regulate the dealings between the union and the boss
• The union as a voluntary institution, with membership rules, bylaws and, of course, elections. All of these internal procedures are carefully regulated by the government
• The union as an employer and property owner

Let's look briefly at some of the most important laws, concentrating on those sections which have the most immediate application to your local union.

The National Labor Relations Act (NLRA). If you are a "private sector" union, representing workers in a private operation, then you, your members, and your boss, are covered by this comprehensive law, developed over more than 80 years. The NLRA is an enormous body of law which covers the relations between p r i v a t e s e c t o r bosses and their unions, as well as relations among union officers and their members (the famous Duty of Fair Representation).

Originally passed as a federal law in 1935, and also known as The Wagner Act, this law was supposed to "level the playing field" by giving, for the first time in the United States, federal support for workers' rights to engage in concerted activities—that is, unionization. The law is enforced by the National Labor Relations Board (NLRB), an independent political agency of the federal government.

As a reflection of the strong anti-union movement after World War II, the act was amended to include the Taft-Hartley Act, which provided restrictions on unions' use of secondary boycotts, outlawed the closed shop and let states become open shop.

One aspect of the Taft-Hartley Law that should not mean much has unfortunately become a HUGE issue after the 2019 UAW-GM strike, because Taft-Hartley Act prohibits employers from engaging in bribery, graft, conflict of interest payments, and other prohibited transactions with union officials. The act is to ensure union officials are working on behalf of the members, so the sorry spectacle of 13 criminal charges and 11 guilty pleas among former Fiat-Chrysler Automobiles (FCA) executives and UAW leaders was outrageous, followed by the suspension and resignation of UAW President Gary Jones and the investigation of his predecessor Dennis Williams. If you are reading this book, I hope it's not necessary to tell you not to take money from the boss in exchange for selling out your members.

Then Congress passed the Landrum-Griffin Act (1959), misnamed The Labor-Management Reporting and Disclosure Act (LMRDA)—misnamed because your boss doesn't have to disclose a thing while the union has to expose every bit of its activity—to regulate internal union affairs, like the local union election which you just won.

Like the US Constitution, which is regularly interpreted by the US Supreme Court, the NLRA is also impacted by "case law," so the application of this law changes almost daily. "The Board" can even change contracts that have been bargained between your union and your boss, with the effect of weakening your union. As justices are appointed to the Supreme Court for their political beliefs and loyalties, so members are named to the NLRB, or appointed to the key position as General Counsel, for their positions on unionism. Is it a surprise that the current General Counsel, Peter B. Robb, is from an anti-union law firm and was the main lawyer who helped bust the PATCO strike in 1981?

Most union members are totally unaware of The Board, and the political backgrounds of its five appointed members. Is this a topic you could discuss with any of your co-workers who thought Donald Trump would drain the swamp?

Since decisions are issued every week, and since the political leanings of The Board affect its every move, you need to keep up on these changes on their website (https://nlrb.gov/reports/nlrb-case-activity-reports). The Board publishes weekly summaries of new decisions and other administrative material. It is a constantly changing world, as you will see, so you have to concentrate just to keep up. If you can, try to develop a *reliable* legal friend, who understands the needs of your local.

One area in which you will find The Board helpful is in its regular offer of advice through your NLRB Region. Check the NLRB web page for contact information. Each region assigns a staff person to be the Officer of the Day, and you can call directly and get a question answered or guidance on the latest interpretation of federal policy. Of course, calling The Board is a little like calling the IRS—the opinion you get often depends on the expertise of the Officer of the Day, but at least you can start with this phone call. As a rule, The Board staff people do not have political agendas and will offer competent information.

The best example of Board interference in union activities involves the union security clause, if you have one, in your union contract. The original Wagner Act did not restrict the rights of the union to negotiate union shop clauses in a contract. A union shop clause simply requires that any new hire join the union after a certain number of days as a condition of continued employment.

Union security should not—but often is—confused with a *closed shop*, which meant that workers in many industries had to already be a member of a union before being hired. The closed shop was made illegal by the

Taft-Hartley Act in 1947. Not only did the Taft-Hartley Act eliminate the closed shop, its infamous Section 14(b) also permitted individual states to pass a state law prohibiting even union security agreements. This obscure clause was the basis for open shop, or "Right-to-Work" laws, which are now in effect in 27 states, a symbol of the continuing anti-union political movements in the U.S.

In states where union security agreements are legal, however, the Board continued to chip away at union strength. In a 1963 decision involving General Motors, The Board ruled that a worker did not have to actually join a union to continue working at a place with a union shop agreement, but simply had to pay an *agency fee* in the amount of full union dues. In a 1988 case, involving a CWA member named Harry Beck, The Board ruled that a worker had only to pay a service fee for union activities relating to the negotiation and enforcement of the union contract. This decision created a *financial core member*, who pays a prorated share of dues even though the language of your union contract says that a worker has to become a member of the union.

Unfair? You bet.

A greater difficulty arises when The Board, or the Department of Labor—which enforces some provisions of the Labor Management Recording and Disclosure Act—makes periodic moves to require that the officers of the union notify all workers covered by the contract of their "rights" to be financial core members, or to pay reduced union dues, under the *Beck* decision. Various decisions from The Board, as well as administrative actions, constantly change these notice requirements which need to be met. Sometimes the DOL accepts a notice published by your international union, and sometimes there is a local requirement which you—as a local officer—must fulfill.

DUTY OF FAIR REPRESENTATION

❖ Source is the National Labor Relations Act ("NLRA")

❖ Derived from the Union's role as the exclusive bargaining representative of all employees within a bargaining unit.

❖ Union must represent all bargaining unit employees, regardless of whether they are members or non-members.

❖ Union shall not act in an arbitrary, bad faith or discriminatory manner with respect to any bargaining unit employee.

14

A worker who does not become a member of the union loses a great deal of power, giving up the right to participate in all union activities such as voting on a contract, attending union meetings or running for union office, and more. At the same time, the Duty of Fair Representation section of the NLRA requires that every non-member be represented if there is a possible violation of the union contract.

Unfair? You bet. Again.

Once again, you need to learn and to study on this area and force your members to recognize this reality in their world and to make it a political issue at election time. Your union lawyer may help you understand The Board, especially since many union lawyers—and most of the bosses' lawyers—worked for The Board at one time, gaining both valuable experience and some important personal contacts.

For new officers in public sector unions, membership can also be a very important—and very complicated—issue: until 2018, it was accurate that state laws or local bargaining ordinances impacted the union's obligation to represent non-members. The ability of the union to generate dues, or agency fees—income to pay for representation—was dependent on both the laws and the union's bargaining power. In 22 states, unions had politically negotiated a "fair share" provision so that non-members had to pay partial dues as a condition of employment.

That all changed on June 27, 2018, when the Supreme Court issued a 5-4 decision on *Janus v AFSCME*, ruling that "fair share" provisions were somehow a violation of the US Constitution. A huge anti-union movement, well-funded by right-wing groups, immediately set out to encourage dissidents to drop out.

Open shop contract clauses, however, can provide a wonderful internal organizing incentive because involving the existing membership will certainly recruit new members. In my experience, workers in these public sector unions vote, so to speak, with their feet. When there is aggressive leadership, membership numbers increase; when the officers are careless, divisive or indifferent, membership drops.

One of the most important elements of The Servicing Model of Unionism is officers who have no fundamental understanding of the laws that affect unionism. Their biggest failure is their pathetic reliance on the union's lawyers for every decision. Lawyers know the law, but they do not, as a rule, understand organizing around grievances or how to negotiate a new contract, or how to administer a local union, and should not be given these responsibilities.

I WANT THE UNION TO GIVE ME ALL THE BENEFITS OF MEMBERSHIP...

...BUT I DON'T WANT TO HAVE TO PAY FOR IT. I WANT IT FREE!

KONOPACKI ©2017 HUCKKONOPACKICARTOONS.COM – DEC

JANUS v. AFSCME

Remember this point, also: lawyers, like everyone else, need to feed their families and, for labor lawyers, a main source of income is the retainer a union pays for legal assistance. By the way, when you look at the union's financial picture, as described in Chapter 6, check out the contract between your union and a lawyer, if such a retainer exists. You need to understand the financial implications of your legal representation— what is covered by the retainer, and what costs extra, and how much.

At any rate, a lawyer really operates on a financial relationship with the officers of the local union, and usually will not jeopardize his/her income by offering a legal opinion in public to contradict the local officers. Many new officers have been shocked to hear some incredible double-speak from a lawyer, either in negotiations or in a grievance or in an opinion, for example, on local election procedures.

You do wonder: What can they be thinking?

The lawyer is simply following one path of self-preservation. Since workers are trained to feel inadequate when dealing with legal issues, usually the response is to simply trust the lawyer. There are some very fine union lawyers, with a lot of integrity, but you need to calculate exactly how far you can trust the one *you* are paying.

If a lawyer works directly for the union, as a kind of fulltime staff employee, the lawyer generally feels—in true Servicing Model unionism—that he/she works for the principal union officer, and not for the members— or for The Union as a whole—and will work to provide job security for both the officer and the lawyer by supporting, with legal opinions, the direction of this officer.

There are outside groups, such as the Association for Union Democracy (http://www.aud2.uniondemocracy. org/), which will help you out with certain internal union procedures, and will try to focus your legal disputes on increased membership involvement.

The federal Department of Labor (DOL) overlaps the jurisdiction of The Board in many areas and is concerned with internal union activities, like financial and election issues, through its Office of Labor-Management Standards (OLMS) (http://www.dol.gov/olms/). The DOL has an enormous website and also issues a series of pamphlets on its procedures and runs webinars on important topics. Clearly the OLMS, like the NLRB, is a political battleground—if there is a partially pro-union administration in Washington, the decisions tend to support unions but when the political winds shift, watch out.

One legal area which has unfortunately become much more prominent in the past few years is the issue of bankruptcy of a private sector employer. The laws covering Chapter 7 or Chapter 11 bankruptcies, and the implications for a union, are enormous. The ERISA (Employee Retirement Income Security Act) laws, covering private sector pensions, and new requirements for reporting retirement benefits for public employees, are also areas for potential legal and organizational headaches for a new officer. You may, unfortunately, need to become knowledgeable about The Pension Benefit Guarantee Corporation (PBGC) which takes over private pensions when an employer declares bankruptcy. You may also need to become familiar with laws that cover a Voluntary Employee Beneficiary Association (VEBA), which can provide benefits and is again becoming more common as employers find bankruptcy as a way to attack our unions.

Organize Not Legalize

At the same time, you should not be trapped in the legal system. A great example of workers organizing when the legal system failed them was when Blackjewel, a mining company in four states of Appalachia, declared bankruptcy in July, 2019, planning to stiff more than 1,000 miners out of their back pay. Miners learned in the middle of an afternoon shift that Blackjewel was shutting down immediately and putting everyone out of work. The company did not file a mandatory 60-day advance warning and did not post a bond, required by Kentucky law, to cover payroll. Workers did not receive pay for their last week on the job. Paychecks for two previous weeks bounced and lawyers estimated that each miner was owed $4,202.91.

The miners—non-union, by the way—could have tried to collect through bankruptcy court, where workers' claims are last in line, but instead blocked all of the company's coal trains, carrying more than $1 million of coal. In October, 2019, Blackjewel agreed to pay about 1,100 workers about $5.1 million in back wages.

Finally, a union is often an employer, as defined by the law and you should try to make your local a model employer. Workers employed by the union often have a union contract, so most of their terms and conditions of employment are negotiated. Even if the employees of your union do not have such a union contract, they are entitled to all legal protections we expect at work. They must be covered, for example, by Workers' Compensation and OSHA, and may be entitled to the protection of The Family and Medical Leave Act (FMLA) if there are 50 or more employees, so the officers of the union need to be familiar with the laws.

Union employees are potentially difficult for a new officer to deal with since they are often politically connected to a current or past officer. A change in administration can threaten their employment, so you need to try to set up a standard for employment based upon skill and commitment rather than political allegiances. An unhappy staff person can be a seriously disruptive element for your local, so treating a worker for the union as you want to be treated by your boss—work, not favoritism—with a clear set of work assignments and expectations, is the best you can begin to make out of an often bad situation.

All in all, the whole area of legal obligations is complex, tangled and constantly changing. It is an area where you, as an officer, must pay attention and it is usually an area where you have the least preparation. The best solution is to take a Labor Law course or to find someone who really knows this area, and learn as much as you can as fast as you can.

Finally, even though your union lawyer can provide legal advice, it is essential that strategic decisions—when to bargain, how to file an effective grievance—should be made by the officers and members of the local. It is simply a matter of good union practice.

Now Go Do It!

TASKS:

1) Get a copy of the full National Labor Relations Act and pay careful attention to the National Labor Relations Board's weekly updates.

2) Get copies from the Labor Department of the most recent LM filings from your union, so you can see what information is legally required. Keep checking the DOL website for changes.

3) Get a list of all legal proceedings involving your union for the past two years, especially if there has been a controversial or expensive case.

4) Consider sponsoring a one-day short course in labor law for all of your union officers, including stewards and members. Having this class on a Saturday will cut your expenses and will serve to increase membership involvement. Better yet, find a full course in labor law because it is something you will use every day.

5) Try to get a good, readable book on labor law if you can't find a class. Two good ones are Bruce S. Feldacker and Michael J. Hayes, A Labor Guide to Labor Law or Douglas L. Leslie, Labor Law in a Nutshell. The BNA Labor Report also provides current material.

6) There is a great book, The Legal Rights of Union Stewards, by Robert L. Schwartz, that covers the topic of union stewards in detail.

7) Look for employment law guides, like Deskbook of Employment Law or Your Rights in the Workplace by Barbara Repa.

${E}$ND NOTE — GO FOR IT!

This final note is more of a pep talk to encourage you to get started and to not worry about making a mistake. As I do union training, I always start by flashing a picture of John Wayne as Rooster Cogburn to illustrate the importance of True Grit, emphasizing that if a union officer doesn't have True Grit, no amount of instruction can help. If there were a Wizard of Oz, each of us could get a heart, a brain and some courage. In real life, you have to create these qualities in yourself and be confident of your success.

If you are doing your best to build your union and increase membership participation, only good things will happen in the long run. The short ride may be a little bumpy, but in the long term, you will be successful.

Consider the alternative—no more unions for us and for our children. We are passing along a declining standard of living as our legacy. In Walmart nation, no worker is safe. All around us, we are seeing the signs of the decline of unionism: the growth of income inequality, the disappearance of the so-called "middle class," millions of people with no health insurance or retirement benefits. It's one thing to see these numbers but you, as the new union officer, have resolved to change them.

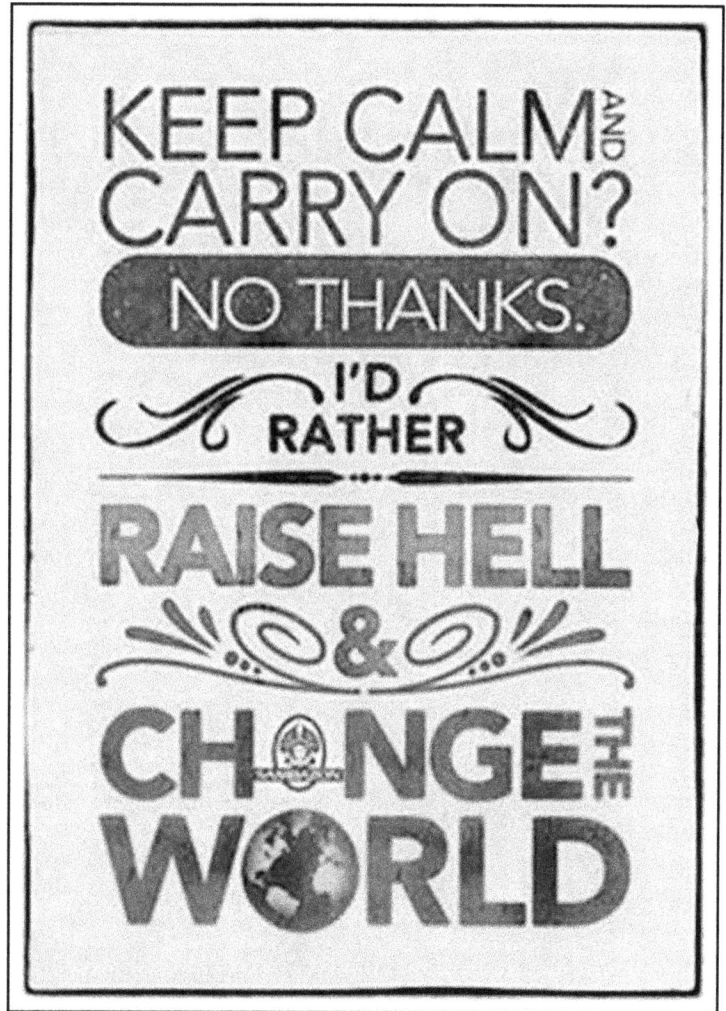

So let's start. Take it one step at a time, be patient but persistent.

And, as Woody Guthrie said, "Take it easy, but take it."

A PPENDIX 1—TWO MODELS OF UNIONISM

When unions were first organized, the workers' success depended on total membership involvement since the early organizations had no resources except the passions of the members and their communities. As unions became more established, this **Organizing Model of Unionism** gradually was replaced by The **Servicing Model of Unionism**, which became the dominant structure for unions. In the mid-1990's, as some union officers recognized the desperate situation for unionism, The **Organizing Model** was revived, at least as a discussion topic.

The differences between the two models are shown below.

ORGANIZING MODEL	**SERVICING MODEL**
Proactice	Reactive
Independent of management	Dependent upon management
Actively involves members in all decisions	Union officers "solve problems" for members in response to complaints or requests
Creates many activities in workplace	Total reliance on grievance and arbitration
Constantly negotiating for improvements	Waits for regularly scheduled contract date
Develops the skills and abilities of the members	Total reliance on union staff, "experts" and lawyers
Open communications channels	Union info is considered privileged and kept secret within a small group
Active membership	Centralized union structure
Bottom-up decisions	Top-down decisions
Regularly supports other unions	Basically isolated from other unions' activity

APPENDIX 2 — WORKER/UNION LEADERSHIP

"Leadership means moving people, moving our coworkers. An elected or appointed union representative is not necessarily a leader." —A Great Authority

Good Leadership	Bad Leadership
Kaizen	Is easily satisfied
Initiative	Passive
Proactive	Reactive
Works hard	Does the minimum required
Self-reliant	Dependent
Self-starter	Waits to be told what to do
Persistent	Quickly discouraged
Positive	Negative
Does not quit	Gives up easily
Sets goals	Bumps along
Does more than needed	Does the minimum to get by
Seeks new information	Closed mind
Absorbs and uses new information	See above
Ready to change	Resists change
Accepts pressure to improve	Resists pressure to improve
Finishes tasks in full, on time	Owns a bagful of excuses

WHICH ONE ARE YOU?

A PPENDIX 3 — UNION MEMBERSHIP IN 2019

The annual report from the Bureau of Labor Statistics on union membership for 2019 illustrates another—and maybe the greatest—challenge for a new union officer. We continue to represent a small minority of American workers and our membership even declined slightly in the past year.

All officers need to understand the phrase "union density"—which can mean the total number of union members in the country, or in your area or in your industry. "Union density" helps to set standards that the boss is afraid to challenge so the lower the density, the bolder they become. Overall union density now stands at 10.3%, down by 0.2 percentage points from 2018, although the number of wage and salary workers belonging to unions, at 14.6 million in 2019, was little changed from 2018.

Private sector density in 2019 was stuck at 6.2%, and public sector density at 33.6%.

By any measure, the numbers of unionism are pretty grim, demonstrating the decline in unionism that has been going on for at least 70 years. Unions have dropped from 37% of the workforce in the late 1950's, and 20.1 % in 1983 when the Department of Labor started keeping count, down to the 10.3 % in 2019.

In the private sector, union members were 24.2% of the workforce in 1973 but today only 6.2 per cent of the work force, a figure comparable to 1900. Total membership in the private sector was 7.5 million and with another 7.1 million public sector workers in 2019.

We represent the same 14 million that were members at the end of World War II. As one commentator stated several years ago: "A generation ago, labor unions were often a familiar feature of the American workplace, but in private businesses across the country, unions have been shrinking. Today fewer than one in 15 private sector workers belong to a union, compared with almost one in four in 1973."[1]

So we have been pushed back almost 120 years in percent of workers represented, and pushed back more than 70 years in sheer numbers. Another ominous statistic is that union membership rates continued to be highest among workers ages 45 to 64. In 2018, 12.8 percent of workers ages 45 to 54 and 13.3 percent of those ages 55 to 64 were union members.

More importantly, the number of workers age 16-24 who are members of a union is only 4.4% and the number of workers 25-34 is only 9.3% so a whole generation of young workers has no union experience.

Some important aspects of this data are:

• Private section union membership is only 6.4% while membership in public sector union is 33.9%, almost six times higher, a figure that has basically held steady since 1980.

• Even though unions represented 16.4 million workers, only 14.6 million workers are members, leaving 1.8 million workers free riders in open shop states.

---

1 Anna Bernasek. "The Shrinking American Labor Union." *New York Times*. February 7, 2015.

- Within the public sector, the union membership rate was highest in local government (39.4 percent), which employs many workers in heavily unionized occupations, such as police officers, firefighters, and teachers. but this strong area of unionism is clearly under direct attack by the anti-union forces, with the *Janus (or jAnus)* decision by the Supreme Court in June, 2018 as a symbol. In 2011, both Indiana and Wisconsin passed open shop laws, eliminating union security and union membership declined by 56,000 in Indiana and by 46,000 in Wisconsin—huge hits for the movement.

- Private-sector industries with high unionization rates included utilities (23.4 percent), transportation and warehousing (16.1 percent), and telecommunications (14.1 percent). Low unionization rates occurred in finance (1.1 percent), insurance (1.4 percent), professional and technical services (1.4 percent), and food services and drinking places (1.4 percent)

- Among occupational groups, the highest unionization rates in 2019 were in protective service occupations (33.8 percent) and in education, training, and library occupations (33.1 percent).

- Unionization rates were lowest in farming, fishing, and forestry occupations (2.1 percent); sales and related occupations (2.8 percent); and food preparation and serving related occupations (3.5 percent).

- Black workers continued to have a higher union membership rate in 2019 (11.2 percent) than workers who were White (10.3 percent), Asian (8.8 percent), or Hispanic (8.9 percent). However, the union membership rate for Black workers declined by 1.3 percentage points over the year, while the rates for other race and ethnicity groups changed little.

- The breakdown by states has not changed much. Over half of the 14.6 million union members in the U.S. lived in just seven states (California, 2.5 million; New York, 1.7 million; Illinois, 0.8 million; Pennsylvania, 0.7 million; and New Jersey, Ohio, and Washington, 0.6 million each), though these states accounted for only about one-third of wage and salary employment nationally.

- Two states had union membership rates over 20.0 % in 2019: Hawaii (23.5 %) and New York (21.0 &). Eight states had union membership rates below 5.0% in 2019. South Carolina and North Carolina had the lowest rates (2.2 % and 2.3 %, respectively). The next lowest rates were in Texas and Virginia (4.0 %).[2]

One statistic that was especially important for the 2016 election was that "by 2015, the number of union members had fallen to 14.8 million, and the number of white men in unions to 6.2 million. That's a drop in density from 48.4 percent to 41.9 percent -- just over the last 16 years. That means that Trump did as well as Reagan in 1984 *despite* more of those union members being nonwhite. One reason why may be women who are members of unions. In 2012, Mitt Romney beat President Obama by 20 points among white women without college degrees. Trump beat Clinton with that group by 28 points."[3]

2 Bureau of Labor Statistics Report. January 18, 2019.

3 Phillip Bump. "Donald Trump got Reagan-like support from union households." *The Washington Post.*

By one estimate, "About one-third of the union's [United Auto Workers] members cast a vote for Mr. Trump and another 8% either didn't vote for president or went with a third-party candidate, breaking from historical trends."[4]

It is clear that there is a movement is to eliminate unionism completely in the United State, and there have been a succession of close calls over the past few years, where the relentless drive was almost successful.

There are several strategies a new local officer can develop from these figures. Obviously, there is an absolute necessity for organizing, both new organizing and internal organizing. Since there are 1.8 million free riders, setting up a program in every unit of every local to get to 100% is essential and should become as much a part of local union activity as processing grievances. Building a strong local union, with lots of activities that involve all the workers in your bargaining unit, is the best defense—workers should want to join the local even if it is no longer required. If workers feel like *members,* and not just *dues-payers*, your union will be so much stronger.

Opening the discussion with your district and international union about new organizing—with the "who does and who pays"—part is important as well. BLS figures demonstrate that the median weekly pay for a union worker was $1,051. While a non-union worker earned only $860, or about 82% and certainly a lot more than any worker would pay in union dues. Create an organizing leaflet like *The Cash Value of My Union Contract* and use it to recruit new organizing leads.

Looking at bringing younger members into union participation in your local is also important. Yes, they sometimes act like they are residents of another planet, but they are the future of unionism. Create activities for them so they feel part of the local.

Unions also need to take a very hard look at their political action efforts. For public sector unions—who have some level of government as a direct employer—having officials who are sympathetic to union is vital. For private sector unions, the attacks on union security in states like Wisconsin and Indiana that have been considered "union" states show how fragile our strength is. Allowing political candidates to divert the attention of our members from" bread and butter" issues can be dangerous and allows the political debate to shift—as it has in many states—to what workers should give up and not what we should gain. Yes, social issues are important but if I don't have a decent job or health insurance or retirement security, does it matter how many guns I can own?

At the same time, there has been a surprising—and encouraging-- surge of union activity in 2019. The BLS has reported that the number of workers who participated in work-stoppages in 2019 was the highest since

---

November 10, 2016.

4 Cristina Rogers. "UAW Working to Organize Employees at Mississippi Nissan Plant." *Detroit Free Press.* July 18, 2017.

1986. Figures up to November, 2019, shows that a total of 575,900 workers participated in strike actions during the year. The total number of workdays lost to strike action is 3.12 million, the highest since 2005. Major strikes by the UAW against General Motors, an 11-day stoppage by more than 25,000 teachers in Chicago, the longest strike since 1987 in the third-largest school district in the US, followed strikes in 2018 West Virginia, Oklahoma, Kentucky and Colorado. 3,5000 UAW members struck Mack Trucks in October, 2019, and the ATU struck against a multinational corporation, Transdev, for 40 days in November and December, 2019. Hopefully these strong efforts will generate organizing success so union numbers will finally start to grow.

U.S. Bureau of Labor Statistics. U.S Department of Labor. https://www.bls.gov/news.release/union2.nr0.htm

The figures of 2019 union membership are at https://www.bls.gov/news.release/pdf/union2.pdf

APPENDIX 4 — TWO MODELS OF POLITICAL ACTION

ORGANIZING MODEL	SERVICING MODEL
Political activities used to increase membership involvement	Political activities restricted to a few officers who attend various expensive functions
Political decisions made by an open vote of members	Political decisions made by a small group
"Political action" means all sorts of activities—petitions, referenda, etc	Political action limited to regular campaigns and endorsements
PROACTIVE—starts early political action, so union can set issues	REACTIVE—political action comes late in a campaign, after issues are set
Really works to build activities	Accepts low voter registration and turnouts
Holds elected official accountable for campaign promises	Timid of offending incumbents and easily "forgives" disappointing officials
"Political work" used to build the union	"Political work" considered 'separate"
Looks for members to run for office	Won't consider running labor candidates
Focuses members on common class issues	Allows "social" issues to divide membership
Emphasizes Labor-to-Neighbor campaign outside the union	Makes no effort to communicate with people
Does more than needed	Does the minimum to get by
Seeks new information	Closed mind
Workers set the issues for politicians	Politicians set the issues and expect union to obediently support them
Looks at all political parties	obediently support them
Accepts pressure to improve	Totally tied to Democratic Party
Understands the powers of the labor movement and makes union issues urgent	Afraid of being "Big Labor" and does not establish union issues in campaigns
Members involved in all strategies	Members only expected to follow orders

APPENDIX 5 — IMPORTANT LABOR LAWS AND ISSUES

National Labor Relations Act

Bargaining issues and restrictions

- Grievance issues and restrictions
- Duty of Fair Representation (D.F.R.)
- New organizing issues and restrictions
- Internal organizing issues and restrictions

Labor-Management Reporting and Disclosure Act (LMRDA)

  Internal Union Activities—elections, ratifications, financial reports, etc.

- Payments to union officers
- Communications
- Internal election campaign issues and restrictions

Internal *Beck* Notice

Labor Organization Information Reports required by the USDOL

- LM-1
- LM-2
- LM-3
- LM-4
- LM-15
- LM-30
- S-1

Who is an "officer of the union?"

Who is an "agent of the union?"

"Featherbedding"

Anti-trust laws

Picketing restrictions

Boycotts—primary and secondary

Union political activity

- Using dues money
- Setting up a Political Action Committee ("PAC")

Using PAC money

A PPENDIX 6 — ATTITUDE ADJUSTMENTS FOR NEW UNION OFFICERS

A man who knew something about leadership, Franklin D. Roosevelt, once said "If civilization is to survive, we must learn something about the science of human relationships." The same can be said for the survival of your union, so FDR could have been directing his comment at new local officers and stewards, who have to look at their personal relations, especially if they've just come into office.

We all have our "work personalities," and in many industries, like manufacturing or the building trades, personality is not an important part of keeping a job. Assembly line workers often are isolated by management design so they can be as grumpy as they want without anyone's much caring. Trades people are hired for their skills, not for their geniality, so a skilled worker will find employment even with a cantankerous personality.

On the other hand, many workers in the service industries, especially women, are trained rigorously in the-customer-is-always-right approach so they have to appear cheerful and perky even in moments of conflict.

In their unpaid times, like lunch hour or breaks, workers create voluntary networks: they eat with the same people, break with the same people and even go outside to smoke with the same people. Often these work groups are self-segregated: by race, by sex, by age and seniority, by language or by skill. It's possible to ignore the workers you don't like or don't know as the work day follows a predictable pattern.

Taking on the new responsibility of a union office means learning all sorts of new skills andan attitude adjustment is among the first significant changes that must be accomplished. This concern arose when a newly-elected officer toured a work site and ran into a longtime co-worker who had a question about the union contract. The new officer brushed off the member, proclaiming "I didn't like the guy when I worked with him and I'm not going to start now."

Officers in service industries, on the other hand, have to re-learn human relations because they will be dealing with bosses who—unlike the customer—are almost never right. Taking strong stands and recognizing that conflict is part of the territory is a major attitude shift for a new officer.

Becoming a new union officer obviously means representing all workers, which may require a careful scrutiny of your everyday activities. Officers must proactively seek out all workers they represent, meeting and greeting longtime coworkers as well as new hires. A shrewd officer will use break times and meal times to circulate, hanging out with a different group each day to break down the segregation, listening to problems from all areas of the workplace.

In an amalgamated local, a new officer should travel to different, and often distant, work sites because this informal face time is essential to building good relations with the members, whom new officers might see only at busy local meetings. With union meeting membership generally low, a new officer might never see these members at all.

A steward also has to learn new "languages" to represent the members. If you have workplaces with different ethnic groups and languages, a new officer obviously has to figure out a way to speak with these workers—maybe through another member who is fluent in the language—and to appreciate the customs of these workers. In order to represent workers out of the officer's home base, the new officer must learn "the lingo" of every area—the work processes and issues, the management personalities and the leadership patterns among the members. Sitting with some of these members at lunch or at a break will help you become familiar with these areas.

One concern surfaced recently when a union officer, a white male, enrolled in a college class that used a textbook called *Embracing Diversity*, and considered dropping out because he thought "there was just a little too much diversity—enough is enough." It is certainly unfortunate for any worker to allow differences among coworkers to fester but for a union officer, it is inexcusable. Part of the attitude adjustment of becoming a new officer is looking honestly at your own prejudices to see if you are creating the same distance accepted by the officer you beat in the election.

And, of course, a new officer has to learn the electronic "language" of younger members, overcoming both an age and a digital divide. You can communicate through e-mails, text messages, or tweets and must set up a local web site to reach out to every member.

Another area of attitude adjustment is a constant sense of the need to learn more about "the science" of being a union officer. At work, we often do the same things over and over, in a kind of routine. If our employer demands that we learn something different—like new technology or new nursing techniques—the initiative comes from above and training is provided, usually on the employer's time and expense. As an officer, the initiative to learn new things—new laws, new strategies, new issues—must come from within or else you will lag behind. No "job" is changing more than an officer's, so everyone needs to keep up with the extraordinary conflicts that came with the Great Recession. Administering your local the way "old Joe" did is just not good enough—didn't the election results demonstrate this?

An occasional training workshop will simply not keep you and the other officers current, considering that all employers, even in these economically distressed times, spend beaucoup bucks training their labor relations experts. If you doubt this, look at the content—and the prices—for management conferences on "keeping your union under control." You should proactively look around for union training classes, get a book or video on union activities and make yourself a better officer, even if it is on your own time and at your own expense. The union—which protects the steward and officers as well as the members—is worth it.

Finally, you must recognize that the status quo does not exist, no matter how much a steward might wish otherwise. The union is either growing stronger or it is being pushed back and the skills and personal relationships of the new union officer are essential to controlling the direction.

APPENDIX 7 — USING THE RECOGNITION AGREEMENT

Ever have a boss throw a grievance back in your face with the happy words: "Forget it, it's not covered in the contract. You haven't got a leg to stand on"?

Even worse than hearing those words is seeing a union steward accept this decision and fail to pursue justice on a reasonable issue—giving up after carefully checking out every article and subparagraph, every comma and semicolon, of the union contract to see if there is some way to get the grievance onto the table.

The fact is that there may well be a way to get your grievance up and running when it appears that the situation is not covered by any specific contract language. Consider using the recognition agreement (sometimes called recognition clause or article). Commonly the first article of every union contract, the recognition agreement is often unknown, or at least unappreciated, even by the most experienced union representatives who pride themselves on knowing every nook and cranny of the collective bargaining agreement.

The recognition agreement is incredibly important because it covers every situation in, around or related to the workplace. Usually the language is deceptively simple: a common recognition agreement simply reads that "the Union is recognized as the sole and exclusive collective bargaining representative (or agent) for the purposes of collective bargaining in regard to wages, hours and all other terms and conditions of employment."

What are "all other terms and conditions of employment"? Just like it says: everything at, around or relating to the workplace. "Terms and conditions of employment" cover the hundreds of situations that arise every day in the unionized workplace. Some of the situations are *specifically* covered by the contract, some are *generally* covered by the contract and some are not even *mentioned* in the contract. That's the beauty of the Recognition Agreement—it covers everything.

Understanding the recognition agreement is especially important because management always tries to extend its control of its workers and its workplace, almost trying to put people under a kind of 24-hour surveillance. There are an increasing number of grievances, for example, concerning "off-duty misconduct"—that is, a worker does something away from the workplace, which may (or may not) be related to something or someone at work, and management tries to enforce discipline. Usually the boss uses the "management rights" clause as a right under the contract to take this action.

Well, the recognition agreement is the union's opportunity to do something similar—to raise any issue as a grievance, whether it's specifically covered by the contract or not.

Once upon a time, a union had *only* a recognition agreement and had to organize to fight on various issues, leaving both opportunity and difficulties for the membership. For example, the original national agreement between the United Auto Workers and General Motors, signed on February 11, 1937, after the big sit-down strikes, was little more than a recognition agreement and a commitment to start bargaining. This single sheet of paper covered 17 different GM facilities and more than 100,000 workers and was language good enough to launch the UAW in the automobile industry.

The recognition agreement is especially helpful when you are trying to resolve a grievance that falls under the category of "just plain unfair" or when you are working through an issue that has come into the workplace since the contract was negotiated—introduction of a new piece of equipment or a new task, for example, or even new ownership.

The recognition agreement gives the union the legal right, both by contract and by law, to pursue *any* issue—repeat, *any* issue—affecting the bargaining unit workers. It is so broad that it lends itself to group grievances, which are helpful in pushing a "just plain unfair" grievance, by getting many members involved in the particular issue.

For supervisors, who are also used to a strict interpretation of the contract, the union's use of the recognition article will be an unwelcome surprise. Many employers hide behind the management rights clause as something that is supposed to cover, in the boss's favor, anything that is not specifically addressed in the union contract. In fact, the recognition agreement is the antidote to management rights. It could well be called union rights.

Employers and unions understand that a contract cannot specifically cover all possible incidents in a workplace, especially as contracts grow longer and longer in duration. Words like "reasonable" and "every best effort" are sprinkled through various articles, and both sides understand that these are open to future interpretation.

Employers fight this use of the recognition agreement, but it's frequently used with great success. One good example involved a critical case for the Communications Workers of America (CWA), when arbitrator Glen M. Bendixsen ruled emphatically in the union's favor in a case involving the assignment of work at AT&T.

New technology led to "new work" at the company. AT&T assigned to management some work the union claimed had "contractually and historically" been assigned to its members. Citing their contract's recognition agreement, CWA claimed the work and the arbitrator agreed. The article specified that CWA is "the exclusive representative for those employees whose job titles were listed in the contract" and for those workers holding new job titles created under the contract.

The language not only helped the union beat the company on this issue but, went further. Using the same clause, Bendixsen directed the parties to negotiate over new work and told AT&T to provide necessary information to the union. These are two areas normally associated in the private sector with "refusal to bargain" charges through the National Labor Relations Board.

For stewards, however, this award offered a mixed lesson, which should be clearly explained to every member. While the arbitrator provided a "win" for the union, his remedy was only a "cease and desist," with no money awarded for back pay or lost work. More important, the original grievance was filed in 1994 and the arbitrator's award was issued in August 1998. So the violation continued for four years and the union members received not a cent in back pay. The point: win your fights by pressuring management whenever possible, not by filing grievances. Avoid arbitration if you can. But that's a lesson for another time.

Stewards should use the Recognition Agreement when filing an initial grievance. It is always recommended that a grievance refer to as many articles as possible in the contract, always using language like "including Articles such-and-such . . ." to make sure that every angle is covered and that nothing is omitted that might be helpful later on. The best course is to also refer to the recognition article as one of these clauses. "The

Employer has violated the contract, including the recognition article . . ." The recognition agreement is the door that opens all of the other articles of the contract, and gives the union the right to raise as a grievance anything that happens around the workplace.

Although the most common part of the Recognition Agreement is for grievances, it can also be used for "Bargaining Between Contracts," or what is often called "Constant Bargaining." The interest of your members (and non-members if you have any) in their union usually peaks during contract negotiations because they all know that they will be affected—for better or worse. All of the workers show an interest in the union, come out to meetings and eagerly listen to any reports. The big problem is that once the contract is ratified, they all disappear again.

Bargaining Between Contracts gives the same jolt of energy and, most importantly, lets your boss know that there is a union. Using the Recognition Agreement, any time your employer makes a change, you should demand to bargain over it—even if you think the change is positive for the members. Your union has the legal right to negotiate over any change in, around, or related to the workplace and should step up and use these rights. If your boss wants to make a negative change—change insurance carriers, for example—in mid-contract, the union should send a written demand to bargain and start up the same kind of contract campaign used during regular negotiations. Even if it is a department issue, spread it through the whole workplace, build solidarity and see your union grow.

A NOTE TO THE READERS

This handbook was written with the help of many new union officers, but we want your opinion to improve it.

Please check out the book as carefully as you read your contract when preparing a grievance, and fill out this sheet. Send your response to billbarry21214@gmail.com

Thanks!

Name_____Local_____

Local office _____How many years in this office?___

What parts of this book do you find helpful—be specific. (Answers like "everything" don't help.)

What parts were difficult to understand?

What parts needed to be expanded?

What parts need to be cut back?

What material needs to be added to the book?

Titles From Hard Ball Press

A Great Vision – A Militant Family's Journey Through the Twentieth Century – by Richard March

Caring – 1199 Nursing Home Workers Tell Their Story

Fight For Your Long Day – Classroom Edition, by Alex Kudera

Good Trouble: A Shoeleather History of Nonviolent Direct Action, Steve Thornton

I Just Got Elected, Now What? The New Union Officer's Handbook, Bill Barry

I Still Can't Fly: Confessions of a Lifelong Troublemaker, Kevin John Carroll

Legacy Costs: The Story of a Factory Town, Richard Hudelson

Love Dies, a thriller, by Timothy Sheard

The Man Who Fell From the Sky, Bill Fletcher, Jr.

Murder of a Post Office Manager, A Legal Thriller, by Paul Felton

New York Hustle – Pool Rooms, School Rooms and Street Corners, a memoir, Stan Maron

The Secrets of the Snow, a book of p0etry, Hiva Panahi

Sixteen Tons, a Novel, by Kevin Corley

The Union Member's Complete Guide, Michael Mauer

Throw Out the Water, a novel, by Kevin Corley

What Did You Learn at Work Today?, by Helena Worthen

Welcome to the Union, by Michael Mauer

Wining Richmond, Gayle McLaughlin

With Our Loving Hands, 1199 Nursing Home Workers Tell Their Story, Steve Bender, Ed.

Woman Missing, A Mill Town Mystery, by Linda Nordquist

THE LENNY MOSS MYSTERIES by Timothy Sheard

This Won't Hurt A Bit

Some Cuts Never Heal

A Race Against Death

No Place To Be Sick

Slim To None

A Bitter Pill

Someone Has To Die

One Foot in the Grave

All Bleeding Stops Eventually (coming in 2020)

CHILDREN'S BOOKS

The Cabbage That Came Back, Stephen Pearl (author), Rafael Pearl (Illustrator), Sara Pearl (translator)

Good Guy Jake, Mark Torres (author), Yana Podrieez (Illustrator), Madelin Arroyo (translator)

Hats Off For Gabbie, Marivir Montebon (author), Yana Podriez (illustrator), Madelin Arroyo (translator)

Jimmy's Carwash Adventure, Victor Narro (author & translator), Yana Podriez (illustrator)

Joelito's Big Decision, Ann Berlak (author), Daniel Camacho (Illustrator), José Antonio Galloso (Translator)

Manny & The Mango Tree, Ali R. Bustamante (author), Monica Lunot-Kuker (illustrator), Mauricio Niebla (translator)

Margarito's Forest, Andy Carter (author), Allison Havens (illustrator), Omar Mejia (Translator)

Trailer Park – Jennifer Dillard (author), Madelin Arroyo (translator), Anna Usacheva *(*Illustrations)

www.ingramcontent.com/pod-product-compliance
Lightning Source LLC
Chambersburg PA
CBHW080626030426
42336CB00018B/3098